Community of FAITH

The Seventh-day Adventist Church and the Contemporary World

To order additional copies of *Community of Faith,* by Russell
L. Staples, call 1-800-765-6955.

Visit us at *www.rhpa.org* for more information on Review
and Herald products.

Community of
FAITH

The Seventh-day Adventist Church and the Contemporary World

RUSSELL L. STAPLES

REVIEW AND HERALD® PUBLISHING ASSOCIATION
HAGERSTOWN, MD 21740

Unless otherwise stated, Bible quotations are from the New Revised
Standard Version of the Bible, copyright © 1989 by the Division of
Christian Education of the National Council of the Churches of Christ in
the U.S.A. Used by permission.

Texts credited to NEB are from *The New English Bible*. © The Delegates
of the Oxford University Press and the Syndics of the Cambridge University
Press 1961, 1970. Reprinted by permission.
Texts credited to NKJV are from the New King James Version.
Copyright © 1979, 1980, 1982 by Thomas Nelson, Inc. Used by permission. All rights
reserved.
Bible texts credited to RSV are from the Revised Standard Version of
the Bible, copyright © 1946, 1952, 1971, by the Division of Christian
Education of the National Council of the Churches of Christ in the U.S.A.
Used by permission.

This book was
Edited by Richard W. Coffen
Copyedited by James Cavil
Cover designed by Edgerton·Bond Image Design/Mark Bond
Cover photo by 1st Light Studios/Dave Sherwin

PRINTED IN U.S.A.

02 01 00 99   5 4 3 2 1

R&H Cataloging Service
Staples, Russell Lynn, 1924-
    Community of faith.

    1. Church.   I. Title.
        262.7

ISBN 0-8280-1421-3

Dedication

Dedicated to those candidates for the ministry
in Africa and the seminary
who have enriched my experience
in both study and prayer
and who now lead communities of faith in
worship and witness.

Contents

Introduction

Millennial fever has grasped the world. There has been a virtual explosion of material from the presses and other media examining almost every dimension of human experience and achievement from this pinnacle of time. We contemplate the end of the great twentieth century—and what a century it has been! But more than that, we stand at the end of the second Christian millennium. One now sees this previously unusual term, with a variety of meanings and connotations, appearing in all kinds of strange places. For us, of course, its meaning is rooted in the great event of our Lord's coming to this earth in human form, and this gives our thoughts a specific orientation.

Perhaps one of the more important functions of the transition from the twentieth to the twenty-first century, which now stands immediately before us,* is that it moves us to reflective thought. We experience this impulse every new year, but it is not an ordinary new year that now confronts us. This watershed in the passage of time compels us to look both forward and backward—to examine the road we have traveled and to think of the course that lies ahead.

Analyses of the past and prognostications of the future are the order of the day. Much of this relates to material matters, such as the great achievements of science and industry, economics, matters relating to environment and population growth and control, etc. But much of it is more introspective. Questions are raised regarding the deeper issues of human existence—matters relating to the relationship between belief and practice, morals and the transmission of values, and what it is that gives meaning and purpose to life. There is considerable literature regarding the institutionalized individualism and breakdown of a sense of communal responsibility in Western societies. It is even asked What, if anything, can prevent society from degenerating into a battle of each against all? A host of recurring questions regarding the essential nature of human beings, ethical questions regarding life and death, the status and functions of religious belief, and epistemological questions regarding the basis of human knowledge are raised in more serious circles.

Perhaps the greatest danger to us in this avalanche of serious study and hype is that instead of allowing this turning point in time to motivate us to constructive reflection about the church and personal discipleship, many may suffer from overload of information and bombardment of the senses, which results in a weariness with the whole matter. It is seriously hoped that this book will not be seen in this light as it seeks to bring some challenging themes to our thinking. It is offered with the sincere prayer that this occasion in time will lead us to creative reassessment and renewal.

The subject of our Sabbath school lessons during the last quarter of this year and millennium, the Seventh-day Adventist Church and the contemporary world, is entirely appropriate to this setting in time. We have thus a coordination of subject and time that challenges deliberation regarding the contemporary spiritual status of the church, our personal discipleship, and the fulfillment of the mission of the church. From this vantage point in time we take the opportunity to look back and consider the growth of Christianity across the centuries and of the special place of the Seventh-day Adventist Church in this pageant of witness. We will review the amazing development and spread of the Adventist Church during this century and seek to understand its global status and presence.

We are also challenged to think of the contemporary world in its wide diversity. How can the church, for instance, engage those in our sophisticated Western secular societies who do not know the Master? And what about those in the great communities of earth that are resistant to the gospel, who have not heard the message of salvation? The church is called to live in this world as a sign of the kingdom. All that it does, and the relationships it engenders, should bear witness to this. Much has been achieved in the spreading of the message of a soon-coming Saviour, but there is hardly room for triumphalism over past achievements. It is the distance to go and the imperfection of our reflection of the Master that should be uppermost in our thoughts.

Reflection regarding the nature of the church is appropriate at this time for an additional reason. The Adventist Church from its inception has been an eschatologically driven movement. It grew out of the Millerite conviction regarding the return of our Lord and early on came to an understanding of itself as an harbinger of the three angels' messages of Revelation 14. Almost everything about the church, in one way or another, derives from this self-understanding. Its function as a missionary movement, the centralized pattern of its organization (which has facilitated efficient propagation of the message), and even its ethos as a community maintaining high moral standards as befitting those waiting and ready for the coming of the Lord derive from this overarching eschatological orientation.

Not surprisingly (given the previously mentioned orientation), there has been an emphasis in Adventism on correct belief—the intellectual side of the faith—and "doing" the work of the Lord. Much has been written about the work of the church, but relatively little about the nature or ontological essence of the church. There are also historical reasons for this. Once the fundamental doctrines of the church had been established by intensive Bible study, the little group in the process of forming the Adventist Church busied itself with the task of gathering the flock and spreading the message. The Lord's business required haste, and there was little incentive to investigate what seemed to be moot points of theology or matters not connected with the tasks immediately at hand.

Now some 140 years later we turn to thinking about the church—what it is, as well as what it does, and how it unites us in the worship of God. The first chapter is devoted to a study of the church. This functions somewhat as an organizing principle for the book. One of the most fundamental questions raised here has to do with the essential nature of the church as this is revealed to us in Scripture. Subsequent chapters will deal with a series of issues that are related to this central concept in one way or another.

It is the purpose of this discussion to facilitate an inward- and outward-looking process of assessment. And this simply cannot be done in a vacuum. It must of necessity be conducted against the foil of the contemporary world and its thought forms. For it is in this world that we experience our discipleship and seek to fulfill our mission.

As committed Seventh-day Adventists we can hardly allow this opportunity to pass without serious consideration of our corporate and individual spiritual standing and discipleship. This should be the occasion for the renewal of corporate consensus regarding our Adventist identity, recommitment to the tasks of the church, and search for appropriate forms of witness.

It is anticipated that the circulation of this book will be largely within the United States, and therefore while the wider church is frequently mentioned, the challenges and specific issues addressed as regards personal experience and corporate witness are largely shaped in terms of the issues faced by the churches in the West.*

---

*The twenty-first century will really commence on January 1 of the year 2001. There will doubtless be celebration to mark that event. However, this will be an anticlimax compared to the January 1, 2000, "happening." The great renewal of consciousness is taking place now, hence this book in 1999 and not in the year 2000.

CHAPTER 1

Images of the Church in the New Testament

The thought that we are a family is one of the very wonderful aspects of the church. The Christian church is the greatest and most widespread memorial on earth. It is a symbol of God's love for human beings and of His desire to hold communion with them. No other institution has shown itself capable of uniting peoples of all nations and ethnic backgrounds into a single family as has the church. And the Seventh-day Adventist[1] Church affords a prime example of this.

In New Orleans on the first full day of the 1985 General Conference session, I was standing on the highest balcony of the vast assembly hall at the Superdome. I had climbed the successive tiers of steps to the balcony for a bird's-eye view of the great assembly. The delegates from the various world divisions were all seated in their places in proper order. There before my eyes was a microcosm of the church—a visible representation of the multiethnic composition and worldwide geographical distribution of the church. The scene engrossed my attention. I studied group after group, looked at their faces as best I could from that distance, and listened to their singing and praying and reverberating amens. The atmosphere and joy of the occasion warmed my soul.

Then a movement nearby attracted my attention. Standing a little to my right was a man who appeared to be emotionally distraught. Moving back a little so as to be out of his sight, I watched him for several minutes and wondered what was troubling him. He was elderly, and looked, I thought, as though he came from Europe. There he stood wiping his eyes, occasionally uttering a suppressed cry, almost convulsed. I thought something terrible must have gone wrong. Ideas about what this could be kept running through my mind. Was he ill? Had he suffered some great disappointment? Or perhaps received news of a death? I did not wish to intrude, but neither did I want to leave a man in trouble without offering help.

Eventually I addressed him. "Can I help you in any way?" I asked.

Startled, and somewhat embarrassed, he looked around. "No! No!" he responded. "Everything is all right."

"But you look troubled," I said.

Then, in a quavering voice, he explained. And as he spoke I could see that his tears were of gratitude and happiness and not of sadness. He lived behind the iron curtain and was a member of a small company that had been suppressed for many years. He had never expected to be able to leave the East, let alone attend a General Conference session in America.

But here he was. He had climbed to the top balcony for the same purpose I had—to see at a glance Adventists from all corners of the earth, who had gathered together to affirm their faith and renew their commitment to their task. All his life he had pictured the message of the angels of Revelation 14 going to every nation and tribe, language and people. Occasionally he and his company had heard of the expansion of the church, but news was limited.

The reality he was now experiencing surpassed anything he had dared to dream of. He had seen the faces of the delegates in the hallways and heard their tongues, as from Babel, in the dining hall. Now as he looked over the whole assembly, the hope of his life was fulfilled. The Adventist Church had become one of every nation, language, and people.

What had once seemed all but impossible had come to pass. The wonder of it all had quite overcome him emotionally. In a

voice marked with deep emotion, he said to me, "We used to
say by faith that the message would go to every people, but now
it has happened. My church has become the home of all people—they are here with us in this place. This is already like the
kingdom of heaven."

Together we stood and marveled and rejoiced at what the
Lord had wrought. We prayed together, and he left to rejoin
his delegation.

As this experience illustrates, the Adventist Church is a
worldwide family of God not only theologically, but in the
practical life of believers. And it is appropriate that we concentrate upon this beautiful picture of who we are in Christ.
However, while the symbol of the church as a family will be
discussed here, this chapter is written with a broader purpose.
Most of the discussion in this book has to do with the church—
its unity, its spirituality, its relationship to other Christians, its
relationship to the world, etc., and therefore the concern in this
chapter is to provide a broad view of the church as a basis for
subsequent discussion of more particular aspects of the church.

It is also important to remember that this book will have a
dual focus: the church and the world. It is not really possible to
think of the church, either theologically or practically, in remote isolation from the world. Almost all the images of the
church in the New Testament are couched in the setting of the
wider world. In the first instance, therefore, we shall think of
the church; and second, we will pay attention to the world in
which the church has its being. As we oscillate between these
two poles, we will do so with the promise of our Lord's return
ever before us. Thus we think of the life of the church and its
twin mandates of shepherding the flock and proclaiming the
gospel to the world.

The citizenship of the Christian is in heaven (Phil. 3:20),
but the daily functions of our lives are exercised in interaction
with members of the wider society. We move back and forth,
as it were, between the church and the world, and in the process we experience a certain amount of tension regarding social

and ethical orientations and the concepts regarding life and purpose. Some may cope with this tension by compartmentalization, moving from one encapsulated sphere to the other and thus living in a bifurcated world. But Jesus Christ is the Lord of the whole compass of our lives. There is no part of our world that can be sealed off, as it were, from the rest. The Christian inescapably needs to work out some pattern of adjustment to the contemporary world.

For this reason the first two chapters of this book are designed to provide a foil against which subsequent themes of the lessons are developed. The concentration in this chapter is on the church—and especially on the images of the church—in the New Testament. The study is not exhaustive, however, and further details regarding the church in both theological and practical perspective will be provided in subsequent chapters. In the next chapter an attempt will be made to outline some of the salient features of the world in which the church seeks to fulfill its mission. Thus the two introductory chapters deal in broad outline with the two foci of these lessons—the church and the world.

"I Will Build My Church"

The Christian church did not come into being simply because the disciples and early Christians felt the need for mutual support and fellowship or a refuge from a hostile world. The church is not a human institution that comes into being in any place merely to satisfy the felt needs of a group of Christians. Our Lord's declaration at Caesarea Philippi, "I will build my church" (Matt. 16:18), signifies that the Christian church was founded in accordance with a divine purpose. Jesus established a new community on earth to fulfill His mission. A perusal of the Gospels reveals the steadfast fulfillment of this purpose from the calling, teaching, and equipping of the disciples at the outset of our Lord's ministry to the Great Commission given to the disciples upon its culmination.

This purpose is revealed in Jesus' teaching regarding the new Israel, of which His disciples were the nucleus. His messages regarding salvation and the kingdom created a community with an eschatological orientation (Mark 10:29, 30). Throughout His ministry the message He taught demanded an allegiance that was constitutive of the new Christian community (see, e.g., Mark 8:38). And His conception of the mission of this new community is revealed in the sending forth of the twelve (Mark 3:14, 15) and the seventy (Luke 10:17-20) as apostles and their empowerment with the authority of the Holy Spirit.

The kind of relationships properly inherent in this new community and the purpose for which it was called into being are encapsulated in Jesus' prayer for them on the evening of His betrayal. The words and phrases that stand out are: "glory," "joy," "word," "that they may be one," and "love" (John 17:1-25). The disciples were constituted a community by the divine "word" of God and were to reflect, as well as give, glory to God. The attributes of joy, love, and unity are postulated as the fruit of their relationship with God and to be realized among themselves as a community. And finally, one of the important results of their love and unity was that "the world may believe" (verse 21).

Images of the Church in the New Testament

There are more than 100 terms, metaphors, images, and analogies of the church in the New Testament. Some are explicit; others somewhat indirect or obtuse. These include: branches of the vine (John 15:5), the ark (1 Peter 3:18-22), the spiritual temple of God (2 Cor. 6:16-18; 1 Cor. 3:16, 17), the bride of Christ (Eph. 5:22-31; 2 Cor. 11:1, 2), ambassadors (2 Cor. 5:18-21), a holy nation (1 Peter 2:9), the people of God (1 Peter 2:9, 10), the household of God (Eph. 2:19), the family of faith (Gal. 6:10), hosts and guests (Matt. 25:31-46), and the body of Christ (Eph. 1:22, 23).

Each of these images conveys a distinct aspect or function of the church. For instance, that of the vine and the branches signifies union with, and utter dependence upon, Christ. Whereas that of the ark signifies the major salvific function of the church.

The bride of Christ is one of the most beautiful and frequently used analogies. It portrays concepts of love, closeness, and purity, conjuring up visions of the final great wedding feast. The image of the "people of God" signifies a called-out community of faith with a distinct identity. It reminds us also, as Paul found it necessary to remind the Corinthian Christians, that the church is "the church of God" (1 Cor. 1:2) and not the church of any person or human organization. The various images of hosts and guests incline thought in the direction of a communal warmth that includes hospitality to the needy.

Each image/analogy points beyond itself to the Lord of grace, who has called His community into being for a purpose, given it a specific identity, and empowered it for the task to which He has ordained it.

The two images that seem to be most frequently employed by Adventists to describe their self-understanding of the church are those of the household, or family, of God, and that of the ark or boat.

The Family of God—The Adventist Church has a strong sense of identity, corporate unity, and purpose. As indicated earlier, it might be fairly described as a family. A family is a primary institution and as such might be contrasted to any limited-purpose institution. For Adventists the beliefs, values, and allegiances of the church are determinative, and not merely factors among others on the basis of which life's decisions are made.

It is not surprising that W. A. Spicer, who had traveled the globe and spent time with Adventists in almost every country of earth, frequently described Adventists as a "wonderful family to belong to." I heard him use this expression on two occasions in my youth, once in Australia and once in South Africa, as he addressed large bodies of Adventists who had gathered to hear him. He was much loved, and in using this term he reciprocated the warmth that bound Adventists together as one. In the sermons I heard, he frequently referred to this wonderful family of God scattered around the earth from Hammerfest in the north to the Strait of Magellan in the south and around the circumference of the globe. And he told stories of the faith and achievements manifest in this worldwide family. Everywhere the family members were united in belief and action, working to proclaim the message of a soon-returning Saviour.

The image of the church as a family is one of the most beautiful and powerful of the biblical analogies of the church. And it is entirely appropriate to Adventists because of their sense of identity coupled with well-defined boundaries of belief and practice as in a well-disciplined family.

The Lifeboat or Ark—The lifeboat/ark image is perhaps the most dramatic of the biblical analogies of the church. Dwight L. Moody popularized this image in a sermon entitled "The Return of Our Lord." He applied the analogy in the following words: "I look on this world as a wrecked vessel. God has given me a lifeboat and said to me, 'Moody, save all you can.' God will come in judgment and burn up this world, but the children of God don't belong to this world; they are in it, but not of it, like a ship in the water."[2]

As is evident from this quotation, by the time of Moody a dramatic shift had taken place in American eschatology.[3] The postmillennialism that was in vogue when William Miller preached of a soon-returning Lord had given way to a premillennial eschatology. On this view time is short, very little can be done about the injustices of the wider society, and the church has nothing to do but save souls.

The lifeboat image, which is unequivocally tied to a premillennial eschatology, portrays a fundamental fact about the church and its function in the world. The lifeboat is distinctly separate from the world and has a clearly defined and urgent task to perform. Given the Adventist self-understanding and the eschatological focus of its mission, it is not at all surprising that this is probably the most frequently used image of the church. And this image fits hand in glove with the household/family of God image, for those in the lifeboat are a close-knit group coordinating their efforts upon their single lifesaving task.

These images—the family of God and the lifeboat—are

symbolically powerful, and both represent fundamental and important aspects of the nature and purpose of the church. Analogies, like parables, are wonderful devices for the portrayal of truth, but the messages they portray, while pointed, are almost always limited. It is always tempting to press analogies beyond the primary message they are intended to convey. But the temptation must be resisted. It is doubtless because of the complexity of the church and its many functions and because of the rather specific focus of images and analogies that so many are employed in the New Testament to convey a balanced picture of what the church is and what it does.

The image of the lifeboat carrying the saved through the stormy waters of the eschatological crisis is a powerful reminder to those in danger of becoming preoccupied with the things of this world that there is an ultimate reality which demands attention and that the church is God's chosen instrumentality of salvation. However, a more comprehensive picture of the church and its many functions is portrayed by pulling the many images together into a composite representation of its many-faceted nature. For instance, the images of hosts and guests, and ambassadors, portray a broader picture of the relationship of the church to the world than do either that of the family or the lifeboat. Considered together in cumulative force, each image adds an important element to the sublimely elevated picture of the church presented in the New Testament.

The Body of Christ

An important image we have not yet paid attention to in this study is that of the church as the body of Christ. The apostle Paul utilized this image in his letters to the Corinthians, Romans, Colossians, and Ephesians. In fact, it constitutes the dominant image in his theology of the church. While the New Testament, as we have seen, abounds in images of the church, it is not until the later letters of Paul, especially those to the Colossians and Ephesians, that there is an explicitly developed theology of the church. And this, to a very considerable extent, is grounded in the image of the church as the body of Christ and of Christ as the head of the body that is the church.

The way this image is interpreted—that is, whether the body image is regarded as a powerful metaphor, but not more than a symbolic representation, or whether together with other passages it is held to indicate an ontological relationship between Christ and the church (that is, a relationship indicating the essence, or being, of the church)—constitutes a watershed in theological understandings of the church. We will analyze the significance of this body image for theological understandings of the church in chapter 6, in which the being and unity of the church is discussed. In the meantime we will pay attention to the two most direct implications of this analogy.

Two important dimensions of the relationships ideally obtaining in the church are brought to the fore in this image: the vertical relationship between Christ, the head of the body, and the horizontal relationship between the members of the body.

First, and most important, it is a powerful figure representing the relationship between Christ and the church. And perhaps the most important element in this relationship is that Christ is the head from which the whole body receives its nourishment and thereby grows "with a growth that is from God" (Col. 2:19). The reference here is not to numerical or geographical growth, but to increase in spiritual strength and grace. This parallels the image of the vine and the branches and conveys the profound truth that the power and authority of the church do not derive from human resources. In one sense the church is a human community or body, but at a deeper level it is spiritually constituted and utterly dependent upon Christ for its vitality and life.

In addition to this vertical relationship, the body imagery points to mutuality and coordinated relationships between the members of the body. And because we are still human and have not yet been made perfect in love, it is at this level that the church experiences a perennial difficulty. The most frequently repeated petition in our Lord's prayer for His disciples is that they may all be one (John 17:11, 21-23). And the phrase "perfectly one" is added once (verse 23, NEB).

This prayer has received an amazing degree of fulfillment, by human standards, in the church through the ages. The early church demonstrated its ability to gather both slaves and free persons, high and low, Jews and Greeks into its midst, and it was remarked of them how much they loved one another. And yet, while this internal solidarity and love have been one of the noteworthy marks of the church through the ages, this prayer remains incompletely realized.

The apostle Paul bore the burden of all the churches (2 Cor. 11:28), and a major part of this burden was the tension between believers. He wrote to the Galatians: "But if you go on fighting one another, tooth and nail, all you can expect is mutual destruction" (Gal. 5:15, NEB). And the fruit of the Spirit he describes is a select list of precisely those qualities that make for peace and harmony in the church (Gal. 5:22, 23).

One of the most beautiful passages in the Pauline writings in this regard is the following admonition to the Colossians: "Then put on the garments that suit God's chosen people, his own, his beloved: compassion, kindness, humility, gentleness, patience. Be forbearing with one another, and forgiving, where any of you has cause for complaint: you must forgive as the Lord forgave you. To crown all, there must be love, to bind all together and complete the whole. Let Christ's peace be arbiter in your hearts; to this peace you were called as members of a single body" (Col. 3:12-15, NEB).

The body image remains a model of the sense of mutuality in belief, purpose, and cooperation in service for us today. It holds up an ideal for us to aspire to and to seek to achieve in the power and love of the Holy Spirit. But again, like the other analogies we have considered, it does not portray the entire range of the relationships or functions of the church. It does get first things first. Nothing is more important to the church than its relationship to Christ. Nothing! If this relationship is neglected, the church will simply cease to be the church. And if the church should fail to experience the love of Christ in its fellowship and mutual support, how can it be a witness to the re-creative power of the gospel? Of all the images, the head and the body analogy most powerfully portrays these two primary relationships of the church.

It is no doubt for this reason that this is the image most frequently and powerfully employed by Paul. But it is silent regarding external relationships between the church and the world. Yet Paul was the great evangelist of the early church. In his missionary strategy he directed the new church he had raised up in the major cities to evangelize their hinterland. This figure, then, constitutes another example of both the power and limitations of images and analogies. We turn to another image to fill this gap.

Center and Horizon

I wish to introduce here a nonbiblical image that can serve as a foil in subsequent chapters for discussion regarding both the church and the world and the relationships between them. This is an almost geometrical model in which the church is conceived of as functioning in terms of a center and a horizon. The center from which the church derives its life and thought and power is Jesus Christ. The horizon that defines the circumference of its function and outreach is this present world. The church, while it is yet on this earth, lives in terms of this center and horizon. Christ is the center of the church, as the images of the vine and the branches, the head and the body, the family of God, and the bride indicate. The church lives in relationship with Christ its center and is nourished by Him.

But the church is also an eschatological community. Precisely because Christ is its center it lives in the hope of His coming and looks forward to reunion with Him at the marriage supper of the bride. This eschatological hope gives the church a horizon in time. The universality of the gospel, God's will that all be saved and come to a knowledge of the gospel (1 Tim. 2:4), gives the church a horizon on earth. The gospel is to be proclaimed to the ends of the earth and to the end of time (Matt. 28:18-20).

The church cannot afford to lose either center or horizon. Loss of the center would mean loss of the gospel; the church would then have no reason to exist. Loss of horizon must inevitably lead to an introverted, dying church.

The church does not exist for its own sake. It is called to mission. Indulging in currents of thought, paths of spirituality, and styles of life that privatize the gospel and shut off the Christian and the church from the traffic of the wider world constitutes a denial of the intrinsic meaning of the gospel. Therefore the church that truly rejoices in the gospel is constantly challenged by the breadth of the horizon of service commissioned by Christ. While its heart is warmed by the Christ who is at its center, its mission and sense of responsibility drive it to the furthest horizons of human need. It reaches beyond concern regarding individual need and personal salvation to God's ultimate purpose for all the peoples of the world.

---

[1] Hereafter designated Adventist.

[2] Dwight L. Moody, "The Return of Our Lord," in W. H. Daniels, ed., *Moody: His Words, Works, and Wonders* (New York, 1877), quoted in William G. McLoughlin, ed., *American Evangelicals, 1800-1900: An Anthology* (New York: Harper and Row, 1968), p. 185.

[3] In fact, this is one of the most interesting shifts in American evangelical theology—one that deserves closer study than it has received. On the one hand, postmillennialism, as taught by Jonathan Edwards, was concerned with the future of the human community on earth during the millennium. On this view, the peaceful state of affairs during the thousand-year reign of Christ on earth will be brought about by human and divine cooperation. America was regarded as having a special place in God's purposes in the realization of this vision. Moody, on the other hand, preached a premillennial message of ruin by sin, redemption by Christ, regeneration by the Holy Spirit, and salvation in the kingdom above by a soon-coming Christ. In premillennialism, in contradistinction to postmillennialism, the coming of the kingdom is entirely God's work.

CHAPTER 2

New Persons in Christ in the Contemporary World

This chapter concentrates upon the wonderful power of the gospel in the life of the Christian. It is a power that not only breaks the inherited human tendency toward evil and frees believers from practices that distort their lives, but also inspires and guides the ongoing life of the Christian. By the power of the gospel we are both made and kept "new persons" in Christ.

The power of the gospel to change human lives has been demonstrated in the practical life of Christian communities from the days of the disciples to the present. It has broken down the animosity and barriers of race and status and has united Christians into communities of faith and love in every place. Christian life in this world has taken many patterns—the communal society in Jerusalem, which has been the model for different kinds of religious communal societies; the missionary-minded and ethnically integrated community in Antioch; and a little later the persecuted underground communities of the second century. We could continue in this vein, but whatever the form, wherever Christians have been true to their calling the renewing power of the gospel has been visible.

Not only have individual Christians lived exemplary lives that have testified wonderfully to the power of the gospel, so also have groups of Christians in their corporate confession and interaction. Perhaps an even greater testimony to the power of the gospel than the individual life of love and devotion has been that of the community living out the goodness of the gospel in mutuality.

Christians, individually and corporately, exercise their faith and live out their experience in some kind of relationship to the wider world. This relationship is described as that of salt and light in the Sermon on the Mount. Our relationship to the world has, as it were, a double valence. We experience our faith within a particular social context, and we are called to proclaim the gospel to the world. The implication of this is that we should know and understand both the gospel and the world. In the previous chapter we thought particularly of the church. In this chapter we turn to the world in which we profess and proclaim our faith. We start with the experience of the Gentile Christians of the city of Ephesus.

The wonderful news to these Gentile Christians was that they too were the children of God and that the middle wall of partition between Gentile and Jew had been broken down. God in His great love for us "even when we were dead through our trespasses, made us alive together with Christ" (Eph. 2:5).

This message has two dimensions. The first is that all the peoples of earth are God's children and that God's grace is rich enough and plenteous enough to save all who come to Him. Second, the transition that takes place in the life of the Christian is described as follows: "God . . . made us alive together with Christ . . . and raised us up with him, and seated us with him in the heavenly places in Christ Jesus" (verses 4-6). The clause "made us alive together with Christ" refers to His physical resurrection. This signifies that we are made partakers of the resurrection of Christ, and the figure extends to being seated with Him in the heavenly places!

It would seem impossible to imagine more dramatic expressions than these of the great change that takes place, both spiritually and in our standing before God, when we become "new persons in Christ." The elevated figures of resurrection and exaltation with Christ, here applied specifically to Gentile Christians, are extended in three further figures, namely, the one body of Christ (verse 16), fellow citizens and members of the household of God (verse 19), and being built together into the holy temple, which is a dwelling place for God (verses 21, 22). The significance of these figures, even though they are to be understood spiritually rather than in a literal sense, is profound.

We must confess that these images seem to be overdrawn to us Westerners. Perhaps this is because we are accustomed to literal forms of speech and little inclined to use figurative expressions. The apostle was writing to people accustomed to the use of metaphor and parable, but even so it would seem that he used these striking figures to awaken their consciousness to the significance of the great change that had taken place. Gentiles who accept Jesus as Lord are the children of God no less than are the Hebrews. In addition, it would seem that the Jewish Christians needed these dramatic symbols to jar them into acceptance of the fact that they were not God's only chosen people. God had joined Gentile and Jew together in the mighty deeds of Jesus Christ.

This passage in Ephesians conveys two powerful truths. The first relates to the profound change in both status before God and the inner consciousness of the new person who has put on Christ. And this is solely on account of the grace of our Lord (verse 8). The second is that all persons of earth are God's children. Those who were formerly strangers and aliens outside the gates have become fellow citizens with the saints and members of the household of God (verse 19).

Christianity in World Perspective

With these fundamental truths before us, let us climb this millennial pinnacle of time and survey the growth of Christianity from the small persecuted early church to the largest and most international of the world's religions. We do so in order to gain a perspective from which to contemplate the world in which we experience our personal and corporate pilgrimage and in which we seek to be faithful and effective witnesses. Let us think first of all of the miracle of Christianity in world history and then address ourselves to contemporary challenges.

It is not likely that a historian living 100 years after Jesus' death would have predicted that the small Christian community, severely persecuted and driven underground in many places, would grow to supersede the Caesars and eventually become the largest and most international of the world's religions. But it has. Now with the benefit of hindsight, scholars looking back speak of the two great miracles of the Christian faith—the incarnation and resurrection of our Lord and the rise of the Christian church. And the church constitutes the greatest argument for the historicity of Jesus Christ, for there would have been no church without Him.

Christianity alone, of all the religions of humankind, has succeeded in making itself a universal religion. It has found a home among all peoples of the human race, and where it has entered it has changed almost every dimension of human existence. We tend to forget how recently this has taken place. In his enthronement sermon as archbishop of Canterbury in 1942, William Temple referred to the universal presence of Christianity as "the great new fact of our time."[1]

Standing on the threshold of the third Christian millennium, we look out on a world that is more than a third Christian and upon a Christian population that is growing a little more rapidly than is the world population. In all of this we see the fulfillment of Jesus' words "And I, when I am lifted up from the earth, will draw all people to myself" (John 12:32) more clearly than at any time since He walked along the shore of Galilee.

So successful have been the missionary endeavors of the past two centuries and so rapid the growth of the church in the developing nations that the demographic center of gravity of Christianity has shifted from the Western nations in the northern tier of the world to those in the south, from the richer to the developing nations, and from the older to the younger churches. It is probably true to say that the most rapid expansion of Christianity in 2,000 years of history has taken place in sub-Saharan Africa during the past 50 years. And it is generally anticipated that the Christian church will continue to expand vigorously.

According to the statistics compiled by David Barrett, the

present world population is about 6.1 billion.[2] Of these, some 2 billion, comprising about a third of the whole, are Christians. It is anticipated that world population in the year 2025 will be about 8 billion and that 2.7 billion of these will be Christians. The percentage of Christians will have increased slightly, to 33.7 percent. Furthermore, it is expected that a significant amount of this growth will take place in areas of the Russian Federation and the People's Republic of China, where the breakdown of the Communist regimes has opened the way for freer expression of religion.

We rejoice and praise God for this geographical expansion and numerical growth of Christianity and for the many faithful disciples who have been the agents of this growth.

Growth and Spread of the Adventist Church—Two dates generally come to mind when we think of the beginnings of Adventist missions. In 1874 the small American church of fewer than 10,000 members, a short 11 years after it had gathered itself together as a united body, sent J. N. Andrews to Europe.[3] He was the first accredited Seventh-day Adventist missionary to leave the shores of North America.

In 1894, some 20 years later, a missionary-minded group of new Adventists in South Africa raised and sent £500 to the General Conference with a request for missionaries to open the work in Central Africa. As a result, Solusi mission, the first Seventh-day Adventist mission station among non-Christian peoples, was established in what is now Zimbabwe. My grandparents were among that group. I was inspired, as a small boy, by my grandmother's account of the story. Her enthusiasm was contagious, and I can still see the gleam in her eye as she said, "They had the islands as their mission and the *Pitcairn* to get them there, but Africa is our great mission field, and we had ox wagons, and we had no time to lose." At that time the Adventist Church had fewer than 60,000 members worldwide.

Adventist mission work was subsequently opened in rapid succession in many places—in the Caribbean, Middle and South America, in other countries in Africa, in India and the islands, and in the great nations of eastern Asia. In the providence of God this virtual explosion of Adventist missionary activity took place during the high tide of the Protestant missionary endeavor. More countries were then opening up for missionary opportunities, and their populations were generally more receptive to Christianity than had previously been the case. In addition, many of the colonial authorities had become supportive of the work of the mission societies.

Adventists entered the mission field later than did the other Protestant denominations, but they were driven with zeal, and God rewarded their work. As an example of this, the little work established at Solusi has now spread widely and grown into a church of more than a quarter million in Zimbabwe.[4] The rather localized Adventist Church with a world membership of some 75,000 in 1900 has now grown into a community approaching 11 million. Missiologists marvel at the rapid growth and spread of the Adventist Church worldwide. It has become not only one of the most internationalized of the Protestant churches, but also probably that with the largest percentage of its membership in the developing nations.

Challenges Facing the Church in the New Millennium

Population Growth—There has been staggering population growth during the twentieth century. A world population of 1.6 billion at the turn of the century has now grown to be 6.1 billion, an increase of 3.75 times. And by the year 2025 it is expected to be about 8 billion, five times as many people as there were at the beginning of this century.

This population increase—especially that of the great resistant populations of earth—constitutes a great missionary challenge. There were some 500 million Christians at the beginning of this century. We rejoice that there are now 2 billion. However, the sobering fact is that the number of the unreached has increased from 1 to 4 billion during the same period of time. The contemporary missionary challenge not only stems from this phenomenal population increase and the fact that the number who have not heard the gospel is increasing daily, but is magnified upon consideration of who they are and where and how they live.

The Urban Challenge—The urban challenge now tops the list of missionary concerns. In 1900 there were approximately 300 cities with populations of 100,000 or greater. There are now 4,100. And while world population has increased by a factor of 3.75 this century, that of urban dwellers has increased by a factor of 12.4.

Again, this is not simply a matter of numbers. The demographic composition and character of many of our Western cities has changed dramatically, and now there are vast new cities in the developing world with millions of slum dwellers.

Both of these situations constitute a special challenge to the church. The implications of this growth and demographic diversity are of two major kinds. The first has to do with witnessing in our Western multiethnic cities. The second is the challenge of evangelization and social reconstruction amid the urban slum dwellers in the great new cities of the developing world.

Fifty years ago the colonial authority of London extended around the globe. Today the world is in London—and in all major Western cities. Furthermore, members of almost all the major religions of the world are among us—some vocally demanding civic and religious equality. The mission field is no longer on the other side of the ocean. It may now be down the street or even the next-door neighbor.

Despite the fact that it has been demonstrated to be easier to win some of these new neighbors here than it would have been in their homelands, where the bonds of kith and religious community inhibit conversion to Christianity, we make little effort to do so. In fact, most Christians find it more difficult to relate to and incorporate their ethnic neighbors into their midst than if they were missionaries in another country. Our social ties, community networks, and preoccupation with the everyday demands of life get in the way.

And of course the question arises as to how we can interact

with this mission field at our door. It takes conscious effort and purposeful activity to engage such persons. Besides, introducing such neighbors into the church in any numbers would certainly upset the equilibrium of our comfortable homogenous socioreligious communities. It is certainly easier simply to look the other way. But can we enter the new century with a clear conscience while ignoring this opportunity for witnessing?

The Urban Poor in the Developing Countries—One of the most difficult challenges on the contemporary missions horizon is that of the vast uncontrolled periurban settlements in which almost one quarter of the population of earth subsists. A third of the world's population is designated as the urban poor, and the poorest and most helpless of these occupy these settlements. I have walked through several of these settlements and marveled that life, short as it is, can be sustained under such circumstances. And an almost greater wonder is that there are missionaries living and working amid the squalor and violence of these populations, where the first great challenge is simply to remain alive.

This challenge will not go away. According to projections, we can expect the population of urban slum dwellers to increase from 1.3 billion to 2.1 billion by the year 2025. What can the church do for this vast depressed cohort of God's children?

Certainly the easiest thing to do would be to expel all thought of them from our consciousness. After all, why should we trouble ourselves about these poor souls who seem to have no hope of any kind in life when there seems to be so little we can do? But they are God's children, and those who minister among them do bring hope and show the way to a better life.

This is the most difficult form of missionary service I can imagine, and those who have dedicated their lives to these people need our prayers and support. Obedience to our Master's commission requires that we wrestle with this great challenge and not simply look the other way.

Revival of the World Religions—Another great challenge the church faces is the revival taking place among both the great and the tribal religions of the world. The missionaries and church leaders gathered at the World Missionary Conference at Edinburgh in 1910 were possessed of a bright optimism. In fact, the whole Western world was optimistic about the future during that era. Their report rings with confidence that the gospel would be preached to the whole world, the message would be heeded, and the end would come. They thought that the world religions were moribund and ready to die and that with the advent of literacy the tribal peoples would leave their traditional religions in a few generations and become Christians. Their optimism led them astray in their assessment of the great religions of the world, and they were only partially correct about the tribal religions.

Although the growth of the church in Africa and most other erstwhile colonial countries has been more rapid since independence, the coming of independence opened the way for the revitalization of some local tribal religions. The same is happening in many areas formerly under the atheistic Marxist regimes of Russia and China. The number of tribal religionists worldwide has now risen to 240 percent of what it was in 1900.

Missiologists are not entirely sure what this portends for the future. Will many of these groups constitute cells of resistance to the gospel? Or, as in the past, will this be a renewed opportunity for mission, inasmuch as many tribal peoples have been eminently convertible? The challenge is to study them and find out what can be done.

The fundamentalistic revitalization taking place among the world's great religions enormously magnifies what was already a major obstacle. We have seen aggressively anti-Christian evangelistic groups develop among Muslims and to a lesser extent in cadres of Hinduism and Buddhism. Again this is a complex phenomenon, but it is driven to a certain extent by a reaction against the invasive secularized media of the West, which they regard as undercutting the traditional morals and value systems of their societies, and by what is perceived to be the failure of Christianity to induce a morally disciplined pattern of life or to provide satisfying answers to the ultimate questions of life.

This is a difficult challenge to meet. It forces the Christian community to evaluate its own stance vis-à-vis the values of the wider society. It drives us to introspective thought regarding the extent to which we epitomize the meaning of the gospel in our private and corporate experience. Such self-analysis would seem to be necessary before we invite members of the great Eastern religions to take part in, and share, our religious experience.

Western Secularism and Materialism—Perhaps the previous paragraphs help reveal the pervasive secularism and materialism of our Western culture. We in the church have extreme difficulty escaping this creeping force. Theologically we are theists, vigorously affirming both the transcendence and immanence of God. After all, we are a people of prophecy and affirm the direct activity of God in human history. Yet in our daily lives and even in our spiritual experience, the secularism of our culture pulls us in the direction of a practical deism (the belief that God is remote and not involved in human affairs).

Historians write of the "de-Christianization" of the West, referring to the slow transition from a God-fearing community in which Christian belief is determinative for life to a state in which Christianity is ultimately regarded as all but irrelevant.

One of the discouraging historical trends of this century has been the "de-Christianization" of the former Christian nations of Europe. Those who have grown up in the home of the Protestant Reformation and lived in the shadow of the great medieval cathedrals have become largely non-church-attending secularized people. And while America remains, to a considerable extent, a churchgoing nation, Christianity is no longer accorded the determinative status it occupied in an earlier generation.

All of this constitutes a challenge to the church, and the challenge takes a variety of dimensions.

First, there is the challenge at the intellectual level. Can we find ways of penetrating the armor of the modern secular person? Can we present the gospel in ways that engage and are intellectually compelling? Because thought forms and the status of human knowledge change, it cannot be assumed that what bore conviction yesteryear will do so today. It must be admitted that the church is not doing as well as it should in presenting the everlasting gospel in ways that appeal to the contemporary intellectual secularist. There is much serious work for us to do in this regard.

Second, there is the challenge of what may be called the experiential dimension of the Christian life. The style and limitations of life in this secular age are not necessarily satisfying. The lack of a sense of ultimate purpose and meaning may eventually transcend the satisfactions obtained from finite and short-term achievements, leaving a hunger in the soul. The challenge to the church in this connection goes beyond the teaching of doctrine. Christianity is more than correct belief. True Christianity has to do with the deepest disposition of the soul expressed in worship and communion with God. Many individuals possess a hunger for this dimension of the religious experience.

If we invite such persons to communion with God in our worship services, will they find what they are seeking? Will they feel the presence of God there? Have we learned to worship God with the full depths of our being? Are we united in love and praise? Do we listen to God's voice in silence and pray with all our hearts? Have we learned how to confess joyously our faith in His presence, to rejoice together in solidarity with those who rejoice, suffer with those who experience pain, and help bear the burdens of those in need? If not, will those who feel a hunger in their lives for communion with God find satisfaction in our midst?

In Summation

We bring this chapter on the new person in Christ in the contemporary world to a close with a brief résumé. We have examined in outline some of the great changes that have taken place in the world during this century. These include phenomenal population growth, the rise of many great cities with their urban poor, the fact that Christianity has become the international religion of the world, the growth and phenomenal internationalization of the Adventist Church, the revitalization of the great world religions, and the "de-Christianization" and secularization of the West.

Many of these developments constitute challenges to the church. Others present new opportunities. The challenges are not merely external. Perhaps the greatest challenges facing the church in these last days are those of maintaining fidelity of purpose amid the distractions of the world about us and generating a spirit of worship that feeds the soul and warms the hearts of those seeking fellowship with us.

---

[1] Stephen Neill, *A History of Christian Missions* (Harmondsworth: Penguin Books, Inc., 1973), p. 15.

[2] David B. Barrett, "Annual Statistical Table on Global Mission: 1999," *International Bulletin of Missionary Research 23,* No. 1 (January 1999): 24, 25. All subsequent references to world population statistics are derived from this source.

[3] Statistics regarding the Adventist Church and its growth are derived from the *134th Annual Statistical Report—1996,* published by the General Conference of Seventh-day Adventists.

[4] In a recent census in Zimbabwe, about one in 12 of the general population, or four times as many as actually hold church membership, claimed to be an Adventist. Statistics of this order are not uncommon in many of the nations of the developing world.

CHAPTER 3

People With
the Same Faith and Hope

The Angel and the Gospel

Then I saw another angel flying in midheaven, with an eternal gospel *[euaggelion]* to proclaim to those who live on
earth, to every nation and tribe, language and people. He cried
in a loud voice, 'Fear God and pay him homage; for the hour
of his judgment has come! Worship him who made heaven and
earth, the sea and the water-springs!'" (Rev. 14:6, 7, NEB).

The central word in this chapter is the Greek term *euaggelion,* translated "gospel." And the central concern is that the
children of God maintain steadfast fidelity to, live by, and proclaim the gospel amid the confusion and distortion of the contemporary world, for there is no other way of salvation.

The scripture at the heart of this discussion is Revelation
14:6, 7. Interestingly, this is the single occurrence of the word
euaggelion in the book of Revelation, and the meaning of the
term is here magnified because it is coupled with four powerful
defining concepts: it is eternal; the events of the passage take
place in the last days; it is universal and is to go to every people;
and, more unusual, judgment. We will return to a discussion of
these shortly.

Most of the references to *euaggelion* in the New Testament
are in Paul's letters, and it is in these that the grand and deep
significance of what it means becomes clear. Why, then, should
we look to a text from the book of Revelation—and the single

occurrence of *euaggelion* in that book—to introduce this lesson when there are so many great passages in the letters of the apostle Paul that outline the great truths of the gospel?

There may be several reasons.

First among these doubtless is the great significance attached to the messages of the three angels by Adventists throughout their history. Early on, this passage had an identity-conferring influence, and subsequently it functioned as a guiding force regarding both message and mission. More recently I hear it used in a confirming sense, as an authentication of the identity of the Advent movement and in exhortations to faithfulness. Generations of young Adventists have learned the passage by heart, and the proclamation and exposition of the "threefold message" has been a common theme in Adventist workers' meetings—perhaps more so in my younger days than at present.

Second, this Revelation passage locates the proclamation of the gospel in prophetic time and space, and this relates to our millennial theme. The three angels bear an end-time message that clearly connects the gospel to the work of the church in the last days. The relationship between the gospel and eschatology, so powerfully portrayed in this passage, makes it particularly appropriate to us at this vantage point in time. It constrains us to look *backward* to see what the grace of God has wrought and *forward* with a certain urgency to see what remains to be done. It calls us to assess our faithfulness as disciples in both personal witness and the global outreach of the church in these last days and to think of our personal standing before God in the full meaning of the eternal gospel.

The Meaning of Euaggelion—The Greek word *euaggelion,* which literally means good news, was originally a term for news of victory, especially in connection with a battle. A messenger bringing good news of an engagement would raise his right hand, pronounce the word with a greeting, and all would know that the outcome had been good before they heard any of the details.

The term was also employed in connection with major

events and religious rites in the Roman imperial cult. Inasmuch as the emperor was regarded as being divine, the major events and rituals of his reign were believed to exert an influence on the disposition of both natural and spiritual forces. For instance, the term *euaggelion* was used to announce the accession of a new emperor to the throne, for this was regarded as the introduction of an era of peace and prosperity for the world. Because the power of the emperor could hold back the malevolent forces of the universe, an induction ceremony was signaled as a victory.[1]

It is not surprising that Christians (and some think that this was particularly the work of Paul) took this radiant term signifying victory and the promise of good things to come and filled it with yet greater meaning.

The clearest explication of this in a single passage is found in Romans 1:1-5. In this passage Paul, after declaring that he had been "set apart" (referring doubtless to the Damascus road experience) "for the . . . Gospel" (that is, to proclaim the news of victory) (NEB), goes on to describe the meaning of the gospel. It was promised in advance by the prophets, fulfilled in the person of the Son of God, who on the human side descended from David and was declared to be the Son of God by power by the resurrection from the dead. He is now Jesus our Lord (that is, had ascended to heaven and been enthroned) and through Him we have received grace and mercy.

This description of the gospel might be summarized as follows: the preexistent Son of God took on human form, was the expected Messiah, was put to death for our sins, was raised from the dead and exalted to the throne of heaven; He is our Lord and bestows grace upon those who call upon Him and calls all to the obedience of faith.

Paul uses *euaggelion* about 60 times in his letters. In addition, he uses the verb form "to announce good news" more than 10 times—with a clearly fixed meaning. The gospel is not merely the reiteration of the events, which every Christian ought to know, of the divine breaking through into human history in the person of Jesus Christ. It includes the exaltation of Christ to the heavenly throne as Lord of the universe and head of the church, which is His body.

Neither is it an abstract doctrine. The gospel constitutes the hinge of human history. The whole human situation has been profoundly changed by these acts of God. It is the divinely powerful instrumentality that brings to light the promise of life and immortality (2 Tim. 1:10; Col. 1:23). It inaugurates the eschatological age of the coming kingdom and has shown itself to be the living power of God unto salvation (1 Cor. 15:3; Rom. 1:16). It is both the hope of the Christian and the criterion by which the thoughts of everyone will be judged by the all-knowing God (Rom. 2:16).

The word *euaggelion* conveyed a sense of victory in its public and pagan use, but this is far transcended by the meaning given to it by Christians—a meaning which signified both cosmic and personal victory that had changed the entire status of human beings before God. It had produced faith, works of love, and steadfast hope in the church at Thessalonika (1 Thess. 1:3-5) and so also in every place. The gospel, which Paul also refers to as "the faith" (Gal. 1:23), was to be proclaimed to all nations (Rom. 16:26; Gal. 3:8). It was put into his trust like a costly possession (1 Thess. 2:4) and his especial commission was to take it to the Gentiles (Gal. 1:16).

As I scan the many appearances and uses of this word in the Pauline letters, my heart is lifted up, and I am not surprised that with this sense of victory ringing in the souls of believers, Christianity issued forth to supersede the Caesars.

Euaggelion *in Revelation 14:6*—The use and context of *euaggelion* in Revelation 14:6 is striking. An angel proclaims the gospel; the gospel is eternal; the gospel is to be proclaimed to all the peoples of earth; it issues a call to worship; surprisingly, the gospel includes a warning of judgment; and finally, the angel is flying rather than standing.

What is the meaning and significance of this symbolism? It is in the context of the last time. Hence a *flying* angel is charged to take the message. There is no time to lose. The angel is flying in midheaven, visible to all. The message is universal; it must be proclaimed to all on earth.

This parallels Jesus' saying that this message will be proclaimed throughout the world "as a testimony to all nations; and then the end will come" (Matt. 24:14, NEB). And the striking similarity of these two passages seems not to have been lost on the early Adventists. The gospel is eternal, encompassing God's entire plan for the salvation of human beings. Beginning with the preexistent Son of God, it includes the Incarnation, the resurrection and inauguration of our Lord, judgment, and the final establishment of God's kingdom. That it is eternal signifies its permanent validity, unity, and unchangeableness.

Most surprising to some expositors is the close connection here between the gospel and the judgment. There has been a tendency on the part of some to separate the gospel from any concept of judgment. After all, if salvation is all of grace and totally God's work, what logical reason can there be for a judgment according to works? Not surprisingly the doctrine of a judgment is muted in theologies of the magisterial Reformation. But as has already been seen, this is not the teaching of the apostle Paul. The gospel requires obedience to God's will and a life that is active in the ministry of love. And this is realized in the life of the Christian, not as a way of earning salvation, but as a natural putting on of the nature of Christ by the power of the gospel.

Paul clearly writes about judgment in the specific sense of the judgment of works done by believers in this earthly life (Rom. 2:16; 14:10-12; 1 Cor. 3:10-15; 2 Cor. 5:10; Gal. 6:8-10). And judgment is emphatically included within the scope of the gospel in the message of the first angel of Revelation 14.

Perhaps most striking of all is the figure of the angel. The vision is symbolic. The angel is a dramatic representation of God's people, who in the last days proclaim the gospel to the ends of the earth. It would seem to be impossible to imagine a more striking or sobering symbol of the work of the church in the last days. There seems to be also the implication that the message will be accompanied by a power beyond that of merely human provenance.

And what is the meaning of the emphasis in the call to "worship him who made heaven and earth, the sea and the water-springs"? The Creator-God alone—the God of the gospel who intercedes in the affairs of this world—is to be worshiped. Neither the deities of the mystery cults, nor the beast and his image (Rev. 13), nor any other being is to be worshiped. The Creator alone is worthy of worship.

While this is the primary significance of the passage, there would also seem to be a secondary implication. What about the idols of human achievement and security, such as wealth and prestige? These too must not be allowed to detract from wholehearted worship of and dependence upon God. And what about the practice of worship? Having read this passage and thinking about the majesty of the God of this passage, does it seem that we worship our Lord with the full depth of our whole being, as seems fitting?

Adventists and the Three Angels' Messages

This passage describing the three angels is deeply ingrained in the Adventist consciousness and has substantially contributed to its self-understanding. It is probably fair to say that no single passage of Scripture has served to coordinate and encapsulate Adventist thought regarding the fulfillment of prophetic time; the distinctive doctrines of the Second Advent, the judgment, Sabbath, and the sanctuary; and its sense of mission as has the threefold message of the angels of Revelation 14:6-12.

The distinctiveness of these doctrines marked off the little group of Sabbathkeeping Adventists, which constituted the Adventist Church in the process of formation, from the other Millerite groups. It gave them positive justification for existence as a separate group and a distinctive message to proclaim.

Identification of the message of the first angel with the proclamation of the Millerite movement served to confirm the Millerite prophetic interpretation and at the same time to extend that interpretation of the time to allow for the proclamation of the messages of the other two angels. Identification of their task and particular message with those of these two angels gave them a powerful reason for existence and a sense of mission. And this sense of being a people divinely appointed to a specific task gave impetus to constraints for a centralized organizational structure.

If one adds to the above the conviction that God had given a specific commission and provided guidance to the movement in the person of Ellen White, it is not difficult to understand why this small Sabbathkeeping segment of the Millerite movement became the largest and most enduring descendant of Millerism.

Notwithstanding the above, it took quite awhile for the Sabbathkeeping group to develop a sense of responsibility for a worldwide mission. The task was simply too great, their preachers too few, their resources too limited, and above all time too short—did they perhaps have five years or at the outside 10?—for them to conceive of such a task. Nevertheless, Ellen White reminded them of the wideness of their task and even spoke of "streams of light that went clear round the world," which the little flock found difficult to understand.[2]

Looking back at those days, W. A. Spicer recalls: "James White used to tell us how sayings like that from the Spirit of prophecy troubled the pioneers in those first years, until they got their eyes open to a work for all the world. And even some of us of the younger rank of workers can remember well the time when we, too, had such a limited view of God's plan for our work that we had to be admonished in plain language by the guiding gift of the Spirit of prophecy."[3]

And when the believers spoke aloud of this vision, those opposed to them would say: " 'It will take you 144,000 years to do what you propose.' 'What!' they would say, 'three preachers—Elder White and wife, and Elder Bates—all penniless, with less than one hundred adherents, all of them destitute of money, going forth with a few hundred copies of an eighty-page tract on the Sabbath question, to give a warning message to all the world! *Preposterous assumption!*' "[4]

James White also encouraged the little flock with the following words: "A missionary spirit is wanted to raise the cry more extensively in new fields, and sound the alarm throughout Christendom."[5]

Notwithstanding, they began to rationalize the task to more manageable proportions. After all, the world was in America, it was argued, and there were people here from every corner of the globe. Perhaps the message could be fulfilled with these as a token for the whole.

A note in *Life Sketches* describes this attitude, which prevailed until the early 1870s, and the dramatic change that took place soon after. "Not until the early seventies, however, did the leaders in the Advent movement begin to comprehend that theirs was a mission to the whole world. Even as late as in 1872, the scripture 'This gospel of the kingdom shall be preached in all the world for a witness unto all nations; and then shall the end come' was regarded simply as a 'prominent sign of the last day,' meeting fulfillment in the extension of Protestant missions. Its complete fulfillment was in no way associated with the spread of the Advent movement throughout the world. (See *Review and Herald,* April 16 and July 16, 1872.) But in 1873 a marked change of sentiment began to appear in the utterances of leaders among Seventh-day Adventists regarding their duty to warn the world. (See editorial, *Review and Herald,* August 26, 1873; and many other articles of similar import in the issues that followed.) By the close of the year 1874, this transformation of sentiment seems to have been effected almost completely."[6]

In August 1874 at a joint camp meeting and General Conference session on the outskirts of Battle Creek—the largest gathering of the Adventist Church to that time—J. N. Andrews was officially appointed as harbinger of the message to Europe. The Adventist Church had commenced its journey to the world. And having embarked upon this mission, in full acceptance of the universality of the commission of the three angels, the Adventist Church began to spread around the world with remarkable rapidity.

The reorganization of the administrative structure of the church at the 1901-1903 General Conference sessions in effect turned the General Conference into a missionary society that harnessed the wide resources of the church singlemindedly into a global missionary program. Extraordinary devotion to this task on the part of church members, administrators, and missionaries during the first three decades of this century laid the foundations for the present worldwide Adventist Church.

Our concern in following this history has been to showcase the influence of the Revelation 14 message on the consciousness of the Adventist Church and to point to this remarkable story as a witness to the power of the gospel. It is not our task now to pursue it further. Rather it behooves us, as the descendants of these pioneers, to think of our response to the message of the first angel, with which this chapter commenced. Perhaps as we survey this history from the present pinnacle of time, it would be salutary for us to think of our own personal experience of the gospel.

But even this is not sufficient. The gospel is concerned with more than personal salvation—it reveals God's concern for all the peoples of earth. And this should constrain us to think of the great unfinished task—the unreached groups of people in distant places, those without hope of any kind in the favelas of the great cities, and the neighbor down the street.

---

[1] Buchsel Friedrich, "Euaggelion," in Gerhard Kittel, ed., *Theological Dictionary of the New Testament* (Grand Rapids: Wm. B. Eerdmans Pub. Co., 1964), vol. 2, pp. 721-725.

[2] See Ellen G. White, *Life Sketches* (Mountain View, Calif.: Pacific Press Pub. Assn., 1915), p. 125.

[3] William A. Spicer, *Pioneer Days of the Advent Movement* (Washington, D.C.: Review and Herald Pub. Assn., 1941), p. 100.

[4] John N. Loughborough, *The Great Second Advent Movement* (Washington, D.C.: Review and Herald Pub. Assn., 1909), p. 275.

[5] *Review and Herald,* Sept. 4, 1856.

[6] See White, p. 203, note 1.

CHAPTER 4

United in Love and Action

I have long regarded Paul's prayer to "the Father, from whom every family in heaven and on earth takes its name" (Eph. 3:14, 15, NEB) as one of the most beautiful prayers in the Scriptures. It describes believers as "being rooted and grounded in love" (verse 17) and goes on to describe the love of Christ as "surpassing knowledge" (see verse 19). Paul clearly presents love as the crowning mark of the church and a natural outgrowth of the gospel.

When I read these verses in Ephesians, I invariably turn a few pages to a passage in Colossians. Paul commences with an assertion of God's love for them and ends in a gentle admonition for believers to "clothe yourselves" with the love that "binds everything together in perfect harmony" (Col. 3:14).

These portrayals of love—first, God's love for us, then reciprocal love for God within the human soul, and finally the love that comes to mutual expression within the community of faith—encapsulate the meaning of the gospel. The literary beauty of these passages moves me, but much more so does the depth of the love and harmony they portray.

In this chapter we shall seek to explore the terms used to describe Christian love in the New Testament and examine the manifestations of this love as it came to fulfillment in early Christian communities.

Marks of the Church

Human groups typically have marks of one kind or another that identify them. These may be physical items, such as uniforms, badges, places and times of meeting, etc. From its earliest days the Christian church has had many such symbols of identity.

For instance, there are faded pictures and engravings in the catacombs (which were dug by Christians primarily, it is thought, for the burial of their dead) that bear evidence of their Christian origin and use. Common among these is the fish, which was found also in Christian letters. The derivation of this symbol is not certain, but it is thought that the letters spelling the Greek word *ichthys* (fish) form an acrostic for the initial letters of the Greek words for Jesus, Christ, God, Son, and Saviour.

There are also paintings that depict the parables and other Christian themes, including, most commonly, Jesus as the good shepherd. And there is the symbol of the cross. The latter is interesting because the Christians dared to take this symbol of death, despised by the Romans and generally regarded as a reproach, and turn it into a symbol of victory.

After Constantine and the elevation of Christianity to a state religion, a vast panoply of symbolic forms were developed, which identified church buildings and communities as Christian.

Even more significant are what might be termed sociological items of identity that, while more subtle in a way, even more effectively indicate boundaries which mark off insiders from those who are outside. These include, among others, a common sense of identity, greetings, special usage of words, symbolic forms of communication, patterns of behavior and lifestyle, rituals, and symbolic meals.

Early in the history of the Christian church, as occurs in almost every viable movement, leaders showed an interest in the characteristic marks that distinguish the true church from aberrant and pseudo-Christian movements. At the first major council of the Christian church, held at Nicaea in 325, the four defining characteristics that have come to be known as the marks of the Christian church were defined as: "one, holy, catholic, and apostolic."

Oneness has to do with the unity of the church; holy refers to the state of the members; catholic indicates universality;[1] and apostolic signifies it originated with the apostles. The existence of this definition indicates that there was a concern for unity, uniformity of belief, and the holiness of the church. Much discussion about each of these "marks" has occurred during the ensuing years, particularly regarding the meaning of holiness, which was later applied to the church as a corporate body. Initially the word applied to the individual lives of believers. It was expected that holiness—a multifaceted concept signifying a closeness to the Lord and purity in life and thought—would be manifested in the life of believers.

Adventists may not use these exact terms, but these marks of the church are as applicable to the Adventist Church as they were to the early church.

Love the Supreme Mark (Symbol) of the Church

If one were to think of a single motivating force that could result in these marks, surely it would have to be the power of love—but not an ordinary love. Only the love that originates in God's heart, fills the human soul, and spills over into the human community could produce such marks. Only the love that is revealed in, and empowered by, the gospel could produce a life of goodness that might be called holy.

Jesus certainly applied standards to human life in what are often called the "hard sayings of Jesus," but He had much more to say about love. When the Pharisees sought to trap Him, He condensed the Ten Commandments into two and in so doing magnified them immensely. "'You shall love the Lord your God with all your heart, and with all your soul, and with all your mind.'. . . And a second is like it: 'You shall love your neighbor as yourself'" (Matt. 22:37-39).

This demand staggers the comprehension. It is quite possible to look down the list of Ten Commandments and answer each, Pharisee-like, with a "this also I do." But when the law is thus elevated into unconditional love, an immensely deeper response is required.

Jesus restated the second of these admonitions in the "new commandment" He gave to His disciples. "I give you a new commandment, that you love one another. Just as I have loved you, you also should love one another. By this everyone will know that you are my disciples, if you have love for one an- other" (John 13:34, 35).

Both the sublimity and the difficulty of this command is striking. Perhaps this is the reason that Jesus repeatedly prayed that this love would be fulfilled in His disciples in the long prayer of John 17, which ends: "I made your name known to them, and I will make it known, so that the love with which you have loved me may be in them, and I in them" (John 17:26).

Meaning of the Word "Love"

The English language has several synonyms for love. For the most part, however, we rely upon adjectival qualifiers to indi- cate exactly what we mean. In Greek, however—and this was the language of the early Christians—there are several different nouns with distinctive meanings.

The noun *agapē* and its cognates are the most commonly used terms both in the Gospels and the Pauline letters. This is the word used in John 3:16 to express God's love for the world, which He loved so much that He gave to it and for it His only begotten Son. It is used in the Gospels to express the love within the Godhead, God's love for His people, the love of human beings for God, and the love experienced among God's children. It is God's spontaneous and unconditioned gift of love to humankind. Perhaps more clearly than in any other passage, the meaning of *agapē* as it comes to expression within the com- munity of faith is spelled out in 1 Corinthians 13. *Agapē* is not an independent kind of love; not the mystical upward striving of the human spirit toward God. It is dependent upon God's prior love—a response to His initiating grace.

Philos and its cognates are used less frequently in the New Testament. It denotes the love of friendship between human be- ings—social love, the kind of mutual esteem and consideration that ties friends together. It is stable and trustworthy and transcends the passion and fickleness of erotic love. The city of Philadelphia, Pennsylvania, founded by the Quakers, was given its name, which signifies brotherly love, based on the two Greek words *philos* and *adelphos,* as an expression of the ideal designated by this expression.

The Greeks used several other terms to designate different kinds of love. *Storgē,* like the strong sound of the word, designates the strong ties of affection and mutuality that unite members of a family together in a lifelong bond. It is very rarely used of sexual love.

Eros, perhaps the most famous (or infamous) of the Greek words for love, denotes the strong passionate drives of sexual love. *Eros* is an essentially egocentric form of love that seeks its object largely for purposes of self-fulfillment The concept was spiritualized by Plato and the Greek mystics to denote the upward quest of the human soul for self-realization in the divine, and shades of this found its way into medieval mysticism. Forms of *eros* may be intensely spiritual, but are more inclined to be drives toward self-realization than are expressions of *agapē* love, which at heart finds fulfillment in the good of the other—that is, the purposes of God and the good of fellow human beings.

Agapē love, as depicted in the New Testament, is unique. It is not simply some heightened form of human love. It derives from God and is generated in the human heart by His grace. It enables us to see our fellow human beings in the light of the new day that God will bring. (See 1 Peter 4:7-11; 1 Cor. 13; and 2 Cor. 5:16, 17, which reads: "Therefore, we regard no one from a human point of view. . . . If anyone is in Christ, there is a new creation.") *Agapē* love is the supreme mark of the church. Failure of this love, which is to be fulfilled quite practically, is a denial of the very nature of the church.

Adventists have paid much attention to the message to the church at Laodicea. However, I find my attention drawn to the message to the church at Ephesus, especially in light of our discussion about love. The message came from Jesus Christ, who found much for which to commend the Ephesians. They had toiled faithfully, maintained discipline, endured much, discriminated between the true and the false, and furthermore were "enduring patiently and bearing up for the sake of my name, and . . . not grown weary" (Rev. 2:3). But He charged them with a grievous fault, a sin of omission rather than of commission: "You have abandoned the love you had at first" (verse 4).

Here was a hardworking church, one that had remained steadfast in spite of persecution and that was concerned to maintain fidelity to the truth. This is referred to twice—first, in connection with true and false apostles, and second, with reference to the Nicolaitans, who were apparently antinomians, turning the gospel into lasciviousness and making the law of none effect (verses 6, 14, 15). A single failure is referred to, but that failure lay at the heart of the gospel. They had failed in the greatest matter of all—that of love (verse 4).

He commanded them to repent, and gave them a very severe warning should they fail to do so: "I will . . . remove your lampstand from its place" (verse 5). Perhaps we could describe this as a legalistic church—one holding the tenets of the gospel inviolate and vigorously contending for the faith, but at the same time having lost the love and power of the gospel. But a church that loses this center of its life is hardly a true church of the gospel. It has grieved the Holy Spirit and snuffed out the love and light of Jesus Christ.

The Meaning of Being "in Christ"

One of the most striking features of the early church is the way the gospel broke down social and ethnic barriers, which normally separate people, and bonded them together in a single community. The classic expression of this is: "There is no longer Jew or Greek, there is no longer slave or free, there is no longer male and female; for all of you are one in Christ Jesus" (Gal. 3:28).

Perhaps the earliest and clearest practical expression of this is the church at Jerusalem. "The whole body of believers was united in heart and soul" (Acts 4:32, NEB), and everything was held in common. Those who had property sold it, and the proceeds were shared so that there were no needy among them (verses 33-37).[2]

This costly fellowship and sharing of lives and possessions—and there were doubtless those within the community who had previously been at odds with each other—was obvious evidence that an extraordinary transformation had taken place in their lives. It is little wonder that those who were close enough to observe Christian communities were amazed at how they loved one another. This love ironed out the barriers between rich and poor, high and low, and slave and free.

There were religions of all kinds in the Roman empire, but Christians manifested a strength of allegiance and a corporate solidarity that was new. The transformed lives of Christians and their love and care for one another are beyond explanation at a human level.

The first Christian creed is composed of the three words "Jesus is Lord," namely, "If you confess . . . that Jesus is Lord and believe in your heart that God raised him from the dead, you will be saved" (Rom. 10:9). This is a baptismal confession. I like to picture the candidates repeating these words before being baptized. It penetrates to the absolute heart of Christian commitment. Is there anything more profound and all-encompassing that could be said in a confession of faith?

This has a parallel in the Pauline letters. Have you noted how frequently he uses the phrase "in Christ," and have you thought of its significance? It appears *inter alia* in the following passages.

Romans 12:5—"So we, who are many, are one body *in Christ.*"

1 Corinthians 1:30—"the source of your life *in Christ.*"

1 Corinthians 4:15—"*In Christ* Jesus I became your father."

Galatians 1:22—"churches of Judea that are *in Christ.*"

Galatians 3:28—"All of you are one *in Christ.*"

Philippians 2:1—"encouragement [in our union] *in Christ.*"

Colossians 1:2—"to the saints . . . *in Christ* in Colossae."

Colossians 1:28—"so that we may present everyone mature *in Christ.*"

Permit me to restate the matter. The individual Christian, with the words "Jesus is Lord" on the lips, is baptized into the community of faith that is *in Christ*.

What is the meaning and significance of this terminology? It depicts the intimate relationship between the believer and Christ, but it also conveys a broader meaning. Paul utilizes the term to describe the oneness of the Christian community *in Christ*. The most common image of the church in the Pauline writings is the body of Christ. It is not surprising, then, that he so frequently refers to this body as being *in Christ*. This denotes a high and profound concept of the church.

This understanding and experience of personal fellowship and corporate solidarity *in Christ* has profound social consequences. What else could foster growth in the transformed lives of the Christians and lead them into their costly corporate fellowships? And because of the eschatological hope of the gospel, the community *in Christ* must have regarded itself as the proleptic fulfillment on earth of the final great gathering together of all in allegiance to Christ (see Eph. 1:10, 11). Thus would God's ultimate purpose be fulfilled.

The strength of this sense of solidarity, of being made one *in Christ,* becomes more real to us as we picture the early practice of baptism. Becoming a member of the new community *in Christ* required a dramatic break with the past and a profound sense of integration into the new. This was both symbolized and experienced in baptism.

We are familiar with the major elements in the symbolism of baptism, especially those of death, burial, and resurrection to new life *in Christ* (Rom. 6:3-6). We have not made as much of the symbolism that comes to light in Colossians 3:9, 10; Galatians 3:27; and 1 Corinthians 12:13, 27. Here those who have been baptized have been "baptized into Christ," into "one body," and "put on Christ." There is a stronger sense here of baptism as entry into the corporate body of Christ than in Romans 6.

In addition, there are significant allusions to clothing imagery in these passages. The stripping off of the old self, with its practices (Col. 3:9), and of being reclothed with Christ and the new self (Col. 3:10, 14; Gal. 3:27) were symbolized by the ritual removal of clothes before baptism and the putting on of new clothes. The stripping off and putting on were striking symbols of the tearing away of the old self and the putting on of Christ.

When one considers the acts and images in the New Testament that reflect the experience of the early Christians as they became members of the Christian community, one begins to feel the magnitude of the change in their personal lives, the depth of the transition, and the powerful sense of being one *in Christ* that they must have experienced. One is not then so surprised at the costly sharing of goods, the bearing of one another's burdens (Gal. 6:2), their fortitude in times of persecution, or even their willingness to lay down their lives for Christ.

What more striking example of the power of an all-encompassing love—of divine love and human love, of being loved and loving in return—could there be than the living witness of these early Christian communities?

Descriptions of the Life
and Work of the Early Church

Philip Schaff, drawing on many sources, compiled this composite picture of the early church and its work.

"Christianity once established was its own best missionary. It grew naturally from within. It attracted people by its very presence. It was a light shining in darkness and illuminating the darkness. . . . Every congregation was a missionary society, and every Christian believer a missionary, inflamed by the love of Christ to convert his fellow-men. . . . Justin Martyr was converted by a venerable old man whom he met walking on the shore of the sea. 'Every Christian laborer,' says Tertullian, 'both finds out God and manifests him. . . .' Celsus scoffingly remarks that fullers and workers in wool and leather, rustic and ignorant persons, were the most zealous propagators of Christianity, and brought it first to women and children. Women and slaves introduced it into the home-circle. It is the glory of the gospel that it is preached to the poor and by the poor to make them rich. Origin informs us that the city churches sent their missionaries to the villages. The seed grew up while men slept. . . . Every Christian told his neighbor. . . .

"The gospel was propagated chiefly by living preaching and by personal intercourse; to a considerable extent also through the sacred Scriptures. . . .

"Justin Martyr says, about the middle of the second century: 'There is no people, Greek or barbarian, or of any other race, . . . among whom prayers and thanksgivings are not offered in the name of the crucified Jesus to the Father and Creator of all things.' Half a century later, Tertullian addresses the heathen defiantly: 'We are but of yesterday, and yet we already fill your cities, islands, camps, your palace, senate and forum; we have left to you only your temples.'. . . It may be fairly asserted, that about the end of the third century the name of Christ was known, revered, and persecuted in every province and every city of the empire. . . .

"The Christians were a closely united body, fresh, vigorous, hopeful, and daily increasing, while the heathen were for the most part a loose aggregation, daily diminishing."[3]

R. N. Flew writes: "There is nothing in that Greco-Roman world comparable to this community, conscious of a universal mission, governed and indwelt by an inner Life, guided by the active divine Spirit to develop these ministries for the expression of its message to mankind. All ministries are based on the principle of the universal ministry of all believers, The cup of cold water given to the thirsty, the visiting of the prisoners, the healing of the sick, the maintenance of the destitute at the expense of the community—all are regarded as services rendered to Christ, or in the name of Christ. The sharing of material goods was an expression of the inner sharing in the life of the Spirit, because such a sacramental fellowship, united by allegiance to One whose passionate love always found form in an outward act, could never remain inward only."[4]

---

[1] The term "catholic" should not be confused with Roman Catholic. It derives from the Greek phrase *kath' holou,* meaning "referring to the whole." A little later Vincent of Lérins defined the term as meaning "that which is believed everywhere, at all times, and by all people."

[2] The ideal of the Christian communal society as the truest expression of the gospel in society has remained alive through the centuries and is practiced by several religious communal societies to this day.

[3] Philip Schaff, *History of the Christian Church* (New York: Charles Scribners Sons, 1903), vol. 2, pp. 20-22.

[4] R. Newton Flew, *Jesus and His Church: A Study of the Idea of the Ecclésia in the New Testament* (London: The Epworth Press, 1951), p. 147.

CHAPTER 5

An Open Community

C hristianity is, in its very heart and essence, not a disem-
bodied spirituality, but life in a visible fellowship, a life
which makes such total claim upon us, and so engages our total
powers, that nothing less than the closest and most binding association of men with one another can serve its purpose." [1]

One of the most fundamental questions we can ask is How is
Jesus Christ present to the world today? And we answer Although
God can manifest His power in many ways, He is primarily present to the world—both visibly and spiritually—in the life of the
church. This is illustrated in the life of Jesus Christ. He did not
write a book as a guide for His followers or a creed of things to
be believed. He left behind a visible community to represent Him
on earth. And He promised this community the presence and
guidance of the Holy Spirit so that it might represent Him aright.

Repeatedly Jesus charged His disciples with the responsibility of being His witnesses to the world. He called them, trained
them, and endowed them with the Holy Spirit, sending them
forth to represent Him. "As the Father has sent me," He said, "so
I send you" (John 20:21).

Paul described new Christians as having found the source of
their life "in Christ." And we have seen how frequently he used
that phrase to describe life in the church. This most basic fact—
He is present in His people—constitutes at least a partial answer to
the previously asked question.

Of course, the disciples had the example of His life engraved in their memories. And under the direction of the Holy Spirit they wrote down many of His words and the wonderful events of His life to guide future generations. He left them the Lord's Supper, which they celebrated with solemn awareness of the meaning of His death and joyful anticipation of the coming kingdom.

True beliefs are utterly important, but the determinate center of the life of the church is Jesus Christ. If He is not present, if there is no experience of joy and renewal in Him, if the corporate life of the church is not the fulfillment of a shared experience of His love, the gospel may be reduced to a dry legalism that has little power to inspire and transform lives. And if the latter should be the case, how can the church truly represent the Master?

Broadly speaking, the church may fulfill its task in two ways. It is commissioned to go out and tell those who have not heard. Christians who are filled with the joy of the gospel are so possessed with an inner urge to share the message of love and redemption with others that the mandate to mission is fulfilled spontaneously—a natural response to the Saviour, rather than in fulfillment of a duty.

But there is another way. The presence of the Master within the church, the joy and love in the life of the community of faith, the fervent confession of faith, the sharing of one another's burdens, should fulfill a deep need in the lives of people and constitute a center of beauty and peace that attracts others into its midst.

One of the most notable characteristics of the early Christian communities, from a sociological point of view, was their strong sense of corporate solidarity. On occasion I endeavor to survey Paul's letters in a single sitting, and when I do two concerns in his thought emerge like twin pillars. The first is his zeal to maintain the truth of the gospel. The second is his constant concern for the unity of the church reflected in members' mutual love and care for one another—a unity that extends beyond the local community to the entire church, with its center in Jerusalem.

The focus of attention in this chapter is the local church and the manifestation in its corporate life of the love and joy in the gospel of our Lord. Before pursuing this theme any further, however, it may be helpful to think of the Adventist Church from a Pauline perspective. The purpose in so doing is to erect a background of thought that promotes self-understanding and the recognition of characteristics that merit ongoing discussion.

A Pauline View of the Church

As we have seen, the New Testament and Paul's letters in particular contain many images of the church. The two dominant foci that emerge from these images and that define the church are Christology and eschatology.[2] The church is the body of Christ. This is the most commonly used image in Paul's writings. At the same time the church is the interim eschatological community. Everything about the church looks forward to the coming kingdom. This relationship might be visualized as follows.

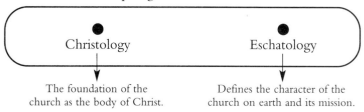

The foundation of the church as the body of Christ.

Defines the character of the church on earth and its mission.

The church in its essential being—what it is in its ontological essence—is grounded in Christology. It is the body of which Christ is the head (Col. 1:18).[3] As we have seen, Paul describes the church as being "in Christ." On the other hand, the function of the church on earth and the horizon of its work among the nations and in time are grounded in its eschatological identity. It is commissioned to take the gospel to "all nations" "to the end of the age" (Matt. 28:20).

The way these foci have been accented and the pattern of interrelationship in which they have been maintained have been highly determinative of the nature of the church. Four distinctly different patterns or types of ecclesiology, each of which manifests a different emphasis on these two constituent foci, have developed during the history of the Christian church. These are briefly described in the sections that follow.

Conflation of the Two Foci—In medieval Catholic thought the church was elevated until it came to be understood as Christ's physical representation on earth. This is clearly indicated by the Latin terms used to describe the church: *Christus prolongatus* (the church is the extension of the incarnation of Christ on earth) and *Corpus Christi mysticum* (the mystical body of Christ).

This view of the church displaced the biblical teaching of God's eschatological purposes. Eschatology was absorbed in ecclesiology, and the church was closely identified with the kingdom. The church was elevated to the status of an intermediary between God and human beings, and priests performed sacraments that conferred divine grace. Being a communicant in the church was much like being on a ferry crossing a river—it would land one safely on the other shore. Along with this went an elevated view of the status and authority of the clergy, which reduced lay members to a state of passivity.

The Reformers reacted vigorously against this ecclesiastical usurpation of the place of Christ in the granting of salvation. In place of this institutionalization of the church and its clergy they taught a doctrine of the priesthood of all believers.

In the view the Reformers reacted against, the two foci were conflated. Eschatology had been absorbed in the Christological institutionalism of the church. In the following two views both foci remain, but first one pole and then the other suffers relative neglect.

Emphasis on the Christological Focus—Some communities of faith have maintained a high concept of the church as the mystical body of Christ. Those who espouse this position enjoy deep personal faith and joyous celebration of the Eucharist, but may have little serious sense of mission. Eschatology may be reduced to a concern for personal salvation and all but divorced from the wider sweep of God's purposes for all peoples of earth.

Most certainly there is a corporate beauty about such communities, and through the ages many Christians have found great comfort and support in them. On the one hand, these churches have been centers of grace and charity. On the other hand, they have often been relatively isolated from the wider society by thick walls and stained-glass windows, which have perhaps been symbolic of other barriers of separation. The lack of an eschatological vision leads to an introverted fellowship, which although beautiful falls short of fulfilling God's purposes.

Emphasis on the Eschatological Focus—Characteristics of communities in this category are practically the diametrical opposite of those just described. Here eschatology defines the character of the church, which is driven by a missionary vision to proclaim the message to the ends of the earth and hasten the day of the Lord's coming.

Such churches are invariably unswervingly true to the message of the gospel and seek to herald it with clarity. There is a beauty to this zeal and fidelity, but relatively little attention may be paid to what it means to be "in Christ" as a community of faith. Corporate experience may wane over against emphasis on individual readiness for the day of His coming.

The church may be primarily regarded as an institution to spread the good news, and it is organized with an eye to efficiency in the fulfillment of the task rather than as a worshiping and praying community. This may result in a largely functional view of the church to the neglect of the ontological dimensions of its being "in Christ."

The Montanists, a late-second-century apocalyptic prophetic movement that proclaimed a message of a soon-coming Christ, exemplify this kind of community. In this movement eschatology was elevated above Christology, and concern regarding the coming judgment gave rise to a legalistic ethic that undercut the assurance of the gospel. Movements of this type have generally had a strong sense of identity but a weak sense of corporate being "in Christ."

There is much that is commendable about such a movement—its zeal in heralding the gospel, its concern for truth, and the individual integrity of its members, born of a concern to be ready for the Second Coming. The general emphasis tends to be on what the church *does* rather than on what it *is*. Expressions of the faith tend to be individual rather than corporate, and Christian experience is fostered more by doing and telling than in cultivation of spirituality in prayer and meditation, corporate worship, and celebration of the Lord's Supper.

Holding Both Foci in Balance—When the twin foci of Christology and eschatology are held in balance, as in an ellipse, there is concern for what the church is—its corporate life "in Christ" as a practical expression of the gospel—as well as for the task of bearing the message to the world.

We see both emphases in the work of Paul. He relentlessly pressed on regardless of persecution or obstacle to proclaim the gospel where it had not been heard. "Woe to me," he declared, "if I do not proclaim the gospel" (1 Cor. 9:16). On the other hand, he not only felt called to found new churches, but also was constantly concerned to sustain them. Most of his letters were written from within one community to another, and almost all reveal the dual concern of defending the truth as it is in Jesus Christ and maintaining the unity of the churches.

He did not indulge in abstract theology. His teaching has the pragmatic concern of building up the Christian communities. His theology culminates in a life of practice, and practice is communal. For instance, the "works of the flesh" and the "fruit of the Spirit" are listings of social vices and virtues that either disrupt or build up the inner cohesion of the churches (Gal. 5:19-24). We see this same concern also in Romans 12:1-15:13; Philippians 2:12-18; Colossians 3:12-16; and 1 Thessalonians 4:1-12; 5:1-22. In all of this Paul emphasized the Christological foundation of the church, even to the extent of calling Christ the church in 1 Corinthians 12:12, and in so doing he repeatedly emphasizes the corporate oneness of members "in Christ."

On this view, both the essential nature of the church as the body of Christ and the eschatological horizon of its life and work are affirmed. The former leads to a corporate life of worship and devotion that reflects the beauty of the Saviour in all its relationships. The latter leads to faithfulness in the proclamation of the gospel to all.

The church witnesses to its Lord in two ways. First, as regards its Christological foundation, the warmth of relationships within the community should so clearly reflect the beauty of the gospel that it attracts fellow travelers into its midst. In this sense it should be a proleptic manifestation of the kingdom of God in history—a sign in the present age that is passing away of the beauty of the kingdom that is yet to come.

Second, the eschatological horizon of its existence constantly reminds the church of the divine purpose in calling it into being. The vocation to which it is called is not merely self-preservation for eternal life. It is to proclaim the message of the final transformation of all at the time of God's great triumph. The church owes the world hope, but it is not enough simply to articulate the message. The church must enter the furrow of the world's need to give concrete meaning to the Christian vision of love.

The eschatological horizon that defines the work of the church also reminds us of a judgment to come. We picture the judgment of the great white throne as the time of God's reckoning with the nations. Or perhaps we think of judgment in personal terms as relating to our own salvation. But judgment will also be an assessment of the faithfulness of the church in the discharge of its mission to the world.

An Open Community

In this section we pose the question What does it mean to the Adventist Church today to be an "open community"? In seeking to answer this, we will return to the Pauline concept of the church as represented by the twin foci of Christology and eschatology, respectively. More specifically, we will enquire if there is anything we can learn from the historical deviations that have either run the two foci together or so emphasized one pole that the other has ceased to have practical significance for the life and work of the church.

Open to Those Outside the Church—Certain scriptural passages refer to openness to those who, whether for cultural or ethnic or religious reasons, are outside the community of faith. In these passages it is affirmed in various ways that all are the children of God and that it is "not his will for any to be lost" (2 Peter 3:9, NEB).

Such texts come to cumulative force in a passage in Romans that reads wonderfully in *The New English Bible*: " 'Everyone who has faith in him will be saved . . .'—everyone: there is no difference between Jew and Greek, because the same Lord is Lord of all, and is rich enough for the need of all who invoke him. For everyone, as it says again—'everyone who invokes the name of the Lord will be saved' " (Rom. 10:11-13). The dramatic repetition of "everyone" in the passage goes a little beyond the original Greek, but it faithfully portrays the meaning of the text. Our God is rich enough for the need of *all* who call upon Him.

The intent is to create an awareness of the openness that the church should have to all regardless of ethnic or cultural or any other human or social barriers. Each of us should have an identity in Christ that transcends all human and parochial identities. The locus classicus of this expression is: "There is no longer Jew or Greek, there is no longer slave or free, there is no longer male and female; for all of you are one in Christ Jesus" (Gal. 3:28).

This openness has two dimensions. The first relates to the challenge of bringing our unchurched friends into the fellowship of the church. The second relates to the possibility of multicultural enrichment in the church. It is frequently said that the time of worship is the most segregated hour in America. Should this be so?

Much about Adventist belief and practice is distinctive. We keep the Sabbath and often work when others go to church. Our standards regarding diet and entertainment, dress and lifestyle, are different from those of society at large. One of the results of these visible and practical differences is that they tend to separate us from the wider society. Adventists tend to have Adventist friends, and even when our employment and daily life are with those outside the church, we tend to live somewhat bifurcated lives and retreat into the Adventist community socially. Our closest associates are generally those within the faith.

Such social isolationism tends to reduce our ability to witness to others. One of the most effective means of sharing the gospel in contemporary society is "friendship evangelism."[4] For a variety of reasons we have not generally done very well at this and could profitably make this a matter of prayer and study.

Increasingly the large cities of the world are becoming multicultural and multiethnic conglomerates, providing a wonderful opportunity for the church to demonstrate the oneness of brothers and sisters in Christ. This may demand purposive investigation of the nature of cultural differences and studied efforts to build bridges of understanding. It is just possible that such attempts will have a double effect. In addition to the affirming function of making others feel genuinely at home in the church, it may lead us out of our Western individualism into the richness of a shared sense of community.

Open to Those Inside the Church—Openness to those inside the church may seem like a contradiction in terms, but sadly at times the sharpest barriers have been those separating believer from believer in the Christian faith. The apostle Paul wrote to the Christians in Galatia: "But if you go on fighting one another, tooth and nail, all you can expect is mutual destruction" (Gal. 5:15, NEB).

Because this also happens in the Adventist experience, I wish to steer this chapter in the direction of the experience of community among believers within the church. In order to do so, let us contrast patterns of relationships in communities that have historically emphasized either the Christological or the eschatological foundations of the church.

In conversation with serious Christians in communities that have stressed the ontological connection of the church with Christ, I have detected how much corporate worship and the Eucharist mean to them.

One committed Christian told me that the experience at the

Communion rail, when he partook of the emblems, identified with Christ, and pledged his life in discipleship, was what really defined his Christian experience. Of course the articles of faith were there, and he sincerely believed them, but it was the feeling of oneness with Christ in Communion and worship rather than formal adherence to a system of doctrine that motivated his life as a Christian. Worship for him was mediated through hymn and prayer, word and confession and silence, and in the beauty of music and visual form. And this was experienced in congregational fellowship rather than in private experience. He did not regard the church as the means of salvation, but it was the place in which the presence of Christ was experienced in fellowship with others. Spreading the message, in his view, was accomplished more by attracting persons into the fellowship than by going out. This particular individual seemed to care more about the experience of fellowship with Christ and communal solidarity within the congregation than with evangelistic outreach.

Consider the opposite case, in which an apocalyptic eschatology is the dominating factor. It must be admitted that there are some parallels in Adventism with historical communities of this orientation. There is great seriousness about the task of spreading the message and preparing for the great events of the last day, but the emphasis may be more on going out than attracting into the community.

Such movements usually have a strong sense of identity—in the Adventist case this is reinforced by concepts of the remnant, the fulfillment of prophetic time, and the three angels' messages, which serve as a badge—and yet the experience within the community may be more that of a cohort of individuals preparing for the judgment than corporate oneness in the gospel.

Perhaps we should be honest enough to admit that there has been a tendency toward a legalistic judgmentalism within the Adventist community. Precisely because the truth of the message is taken with utter seriousness and because of an apocalyptic view of the judgment, any deviation from truth and moral rectitude may serve as a cause for discipline or correction. This may easily result in a tendency toward a legalistic rather than a grace orientation. And it may also undercut the joyous sense of victory that should fill the Christian's soul.

Permit me to give an illustration. A professional person became convinced of the truth of Adventism through the ministry of a friend and was baptized into church membership. But there were incessant squabbles in the church about rather minor matters—aspects of Sabbathkeeping, peripheral matters of doctrine, the wedding ring, and others. These gave rise to a rather judgmental spirit. This member struggled with all of this for about a year, but then gave up and left the church, telling a friend, "I believe what the Adventist Church teaches, but in order to remain a Christian I am returning to my old church." Sadly, Christ was not present to this person in the Adventist community. What can we do to break down these internal barriers and create a stronger sense of mutuality and fellowship in the church?

-----

[1] Lesslie Newbigin, *The Household of God* (New York: Friendship Press, 1954), pp. 76, 77.

[2] I was introduced to the understanding of Pauline ecclesiology presented here by a seminary professor, Paul Beker, many years ago. It has gained force in my thought during the intervening years. See his latest exposition of the theme in J. Christian Beker, *Paul the Apostle: The Triumph of God in Life and Thought* (Philadelphia: Fortress Press, 1980), pp. 303-315.

[3] Ontology is a philosophical term denoting the being, or essential nature, of an entity. There has been almost endless discussion regarding the meaning of "the body of Christ" image of the church. Some regard the symbol as a simple image or metaphor. Others regard the symbol as defining an ontological relationship between Christ and the church. This will be discussed in greater detail in the next chapter.

[4] See Monte Sahlin, *Sharing Our Faith With Friends Without Losing Either* (Hagerstown, Md.: Review and Herald Pub. Assn., 1990). Especially note chapter 3, "Friendship Evangelism: Key to Reaching the Unchurched."

CHAPTER 6

United in Diversity– Individualism and Community

S ir, you wish to serve God and go to heaven? Remember that you cannot serve him alone. You must therefore find companions or make them; the Bible knows nothing of solitary religion."[1]

So said "a serious man" to John Wesley. Wesley had graduated from Oxford, been ordained a priest of the Anglican Church, elected a fellow of Lincoln College, Oxford, and was serving a temporary curacy at Wroote. During this interval before taking up tutorial responsibilities at Lincoln, he was deeply immersed in the writings of the mystics and much attracted to the idea of a contemplative spiritual life. Hence his visit to the unnamed person who gave him the above advice. He recorded this message in his private journal, and Henry Moore, his biographer, says he never forgot it.

The Theme of This Chapter

The centerpiece of this study is the Pauline portrayal of the church as the body of Christ. This image is so central to Paul's understanding of the church and so forcefully drawn that it has occasioned considerable debate about many dimensions of the church. The issues discussed may be gathered together into three categories:

1. How this image is interpreted and what it signifies regarding the nature of the church.

2. Matters relating to church unity; broadly as in the concerns of the World Council of Churches and locally within a single congregation. This image also relates to the question of whether Christian experience is best nurtured in mystical withdrawal or in corporate relationship with fellow believers in a life of service.

3. Matters relating to different functions and offices in the church, including the subject of special gifts, both natural and spiritual, for special ministries.

It is not possible to discuss all of these. Attention will be paid to the two issues that seem to be most pertinent to the Adventist Church today: (a) the tension between individualism and corporate experience in the way of salvation and (b) the question of the nature of the church.

Social Religion—One of the challenges facing the church in the West in the new millennium is our institutionalized individualism. Even in church we worship as individuals without a strong sense of mutuality in the Christian experience. Individualism is a threat not only to the church but perhaps even more to the wider society and its institutions.

Sociologists are much concerned with the phenomenon, and it is the subject of one of the most widely read sociological studies of contemporary American society.[2] The image of the church as a human body with its many members brings what Wesley calls social religion to the fore. This is the reason for beginning this chapter with Wesley.

Upon returning to Oxford, Wesley assumed leadership of the "Holy Club" and embarked on the course of what he called "social religion." According to Wesley inward holiness (personal love for God) comes to expression in outward holiness (love of neighbor). This understanding of the corporate dimension of the way of salvation was eventually realized in the system of classes and bands that formed the backbone of the Methodist revival.

Wesley's opposition to the way of salvation taught by the mystics was expressed in the following forthright terms: "The gospel of Christ knows of no religion but social; no holiness but social holiness."[3]

A decade later he wrote a series of 13 sermons on our Lord's sermon on the mount. In the fourth sermon, based on Jesus' salt and light of the world analogies (Matt. 5:13-16), he affirmed that "Christianity is essentially a social religion." He then went on to develop the contrary corollary that "to turn it into a solitary religion is to destroy it."[4]

He developed the theme by stating that the root of religion lies "in the heart, the inmost soul." It is "the union of the soul with God, and the life of God in the soul of man."[5] True religion cannot be hidden, for Christians are the light of the world. "That the religion described by our Lord . . . cannot subsist without society, without our living and conversing with other men, is manifest from hence, that several of the most essential branches thereof can have no place if we have no intercourse with the world."[6]

"This is the great reason why the providence of God has so mingled you together with other men, that whatever grace you have received of God may through you be communicated to others."[7] "It is impossible for any that have it to conceal the religion of Jesus Christ. This our Lord makes plain beyond all contradiction, by a twofold comparison: 'Ye are the light of the world. A city set on an hill cannot be hid.'"[8]

Wesley was convinced that the Bible knows nothing of solitary religion. The principle he advanced is that inward and outward religion are both necessary.

The beauty of Christianity comes to its highest expression in the shared experience of the community, and worship offers its most inspiring moments in corporate praise. It is within the community that the individual both shares her or his blessings and is corrected, in which the weak are strengthened and the proud kept humble, and in which those who mourn are comforted and those who rejoice share their joy.

As is clear in Wesley's sermon quoted previously, for him the community of faith serves a dual purpose. Not only is it the place in which personal experience is strengthened, but the example of the community as a whole is a living manifestation of the love of the gospel—it is like salt that spreads its savor and a light on a hill that cannot be hidden.

If any should think that Wesley's emphasis upon the importance and functions of the corporate experience of Christianity is theoretical, a survey of the Methodist *Book of Discipline,* in which the rules of the classes and bands are spelled out and a reading of the testimonies of members of these classes, will dispel all doubt. It is probably fair to say that the class experience shaped the personal life of Methodists as definitively as did Wesley's sermons.[9] It was here that belief was translated into practice.

Something similar to this marked early Adventism. The little band on its upward way understood themselves to be a remnant, called out of the world, to perform a special task. This generated a powerful sense of corporate solidarity. They studied and worshiped and prayed together and devoted almost all their earthly possessions to the propagation of the message. Like the Methodists, they organized social meetings, as the classes came to be called in America, for mutual spiritual support.

Ellen White's religious experience was molded in Methodist camp meetings and class meetings.[10] The order she suggests for conducting social meetings[11] in the young Adventist Church is similar to the Methodist rules. These meetings in which members shared their blessings and difficulties and supported one another died out in Adventism toward the end of the nineteenth century. One reason for its demise may be that the Sabbath school class took its place. However, these have been turned into study sessions in which the intellectual dimensions of the faith are elevated above the experiential.

But the difference lies even deeper than this. Study may serve the useful purpose of strengthening shared belief, but it does not of itself pluck one out of individualism as did the social meetings described by Ellen White. "We meet together to edify one another by an interchange of thoughts and feelings, to gather strength, and light, and courage by becoming acquainted with one another's hopes and aspirations; and by our earnest, heartfelt prayers, offered up in faith, we receive refreshment and vigor from the Source of our strength. . . .

"A living experience is made up of daily trials, conflicts, and temptations, strong efforts and victories, and great peace and joy gained through Jesus. A simple relation of such experiences gives light, strength, and knowledge that will aid others in their advancement in the divine life." [12]

Perhaps a consideration of the body image of the church and the excerpts from Wesley and Ellen White can serve to awaken us to the beauty of the corporate dimensions of the religious life and of our individualistic tendencies.

Individualism undercuts the deep and lasting bonds of community. Generally we retain membership in groups only as long as they serve our purposes. Students want to hang free, do their own thing, and establish their own identity. We do not easily notice when our freedom becomes a trespass against our neighbor. The self is thought of as being complete in itself—until calamity strikes. This is the spirit of the age, but it is at odds with the deep human need for genuine community and a sense of connectedness.

Additionally our exaggerated sense of the individual—institutionalized individualism, as the sociologists call it—is quite out of harmony with the biblical witness. The biblical picture of the way of salvation is a way of community—a fullness of life with fellow believers in corporate communion with God.

One Body in Christ

What the apostle Paul writes about justification by faith can be interpreted as representing an individualistic understanding of salvation. However, when the broad sweep of his writings is considered, the corporate character of the Christian experience becomes manifest. Nowhere does this come to clearer expression than in his portrayal of the church as the body of Christ. And it is in connection with this image that the most sublime portrayal of the church in the New Testament comes into view. We shall consider the major passages in which this image is developed:

"For as in one body we have many members, and not all the members have the same function, so we, who are many, *are one body in Christ*" (Rom. 12:4, 5).

"For just as the body is one and has many members, and all the members of the body, though many, are one body, *so it is with Christ.* . . . Now you are the *body of Christ* and individually members of it" (1 Cor. 12:12-27).

"And he has put all things under his feet and has made him the head over all things for the church, which *is his body,* the fullness of him who fills all in all" (Eph. 1:22, 23).

"There is *one body* and one Spirit, just as you were called to the one hope of your calling" (Eph. 4:4).

"He is the *head of the body,* the church. . . . I am completing what is lacking in Christ's afflictions for the sake of *his body,* that is, the church" (Col. 1:18-24).

"And not holding fast to *the head,* from whom the *whole body,* nourished and held together by its ligaments and sinews, grows with a growth that is of God" (Col. 2:19).

In these passages the body and its constituent parts with their corresponding functions are utilized as an analogy for the church with its many members, each of whom has some special gift to contribute. The first great question in the search to understand the meaning of this imagery is Should it be understood metaphorically, or does it rather constitute an ontological[13] definition of the nature of the church? In other words, is the church in some mystical sense the body of Christ, or is it ontologically the body of Christ? Exactly in what sense is Christ present in the church? This is a deep and profound mystery.

If Christians were deists or secular naturalists and did not believe that God is active in human history, the answer would be simple. The church would be regarded as a human organization with specific, but perfectly natural, functions to fulfill. No thought of a supernatural presence would complicate the issue. But we are theists and live in a universe that we believe is governed by God and in which His power and Spirit are omnipresent. This being the case, the answers regarding the mystery of the presence of Christ in the church are more complex, ranging from affirmation of ontological continuity between Christ and the church on the one hand to a spiritual presence on the other.

Several of the Pauline passages quoted previously lend themselves to an interpretation of the church as the literal body of Christ. For instance, having drawn an analogy between the human body and the church, Paul dares to call the church "the Christ" (1 Cor. 12:12). In this text the Greek phrase "thus also *the* Christ" is rather uncompromising in view of the definite article "the" that the apostle uses. It is abundantly clear throughout the chapter that Paul is writing about the church. Why, then, does he call the church "the Christ" in this manner? And he reaffirms the figure in verse 27: "You are the body of Christ."

This figure is continued in his Prison Epistles, most directly in the letter to the Ephesians, which is really the book of the church. Here the church is designated as the body of Christ, and Christ as its supreme head. Paul adds an additional element by insisting that Christ fills His body (the church) just as He fills the universe (Eph. 1:23).

This body image is sustained in the letter to the Colossians, and here again Paul adds a new element—that of growth. Christ as the head of the body is the source of the growth of the living body (Col. 2:19).

Considering the breadth and depth of the development of this body image of the church in these letters, it is not surprising that those with a high and reverent esteem for the church interpret these statements literally. They regard them as signifying a relationship of being between Christ and the church. For such, the church in some indefinable sense is a continuation of His presence.

On this ontological view, almost everything to do with the church and its work must inevitably start from a theological understanding of the nature of the church. This concept of the church is located at the Christological locus of the ellipse on page 59. Typically, worship in such communities is reverent and spiritually fulfilling and easily lends itself to shared experience, but there may be a tendency to neglect those functions that derive from the eschatological locus of the ellipse.

Others understand the apostle Paul to be using the image of the human body with its many interdependent members as the most striking possible symbol to describe relationships—both vertical and horizontal—as they should be in the church. And as if the body image is not sufficiently powerful, additional force is added to the symbol by referring to it as the body of Christ, and even more specifically, as the body of which Christ is the head. Here then is an extremely powerful metaphor, which certainly implies a close spiritual connection but not necessarily an ontological relationship between the church and Christ.

There is a parallelism between "the people of God," "the church of God," and the being "in Christ" terms examined earlier, and the "body of Christ" symbol, which makes it logical to interpret the latter metaphorically. A high view of the church as the body of Christ—the chosen people among whom He is present—may be maintained without the implication of ontological continuity with Christ.

This pattern of interpretation is more amenable to the maintenance of balance between the Christological and eschatological dimensions of the church outlined in chapter 5, and it facilitates emphasis of both the spiritual and external functions of the church.

Toward an Adventist Understanding of the Church

How do we as Adventists understand this image of the church? Perhaps it will be helpful to review a little history before an answer is attempted. Our spiritual ancestors were motivated by an eschatological urgency to proclaim the message. Once the defining Adventist truths had been established, they had little incentive to investigate finer points of doctrine such as the nature of the church. Such matters seemed irrelevant to the task at hand. In addition, many of those who became Adventists came out of communities such as the Christian Connection, which sought to radically reform the church and restore it to the simplicity of New Testament times.

Therefore, definitions of doctrine in the creeds and contemporary forms of church organization were rejected as human inventions that betrayed the gospel. Thomas Campbell's famous "Declaration and Address," the spirit of which is practically summarized in the sentence "Where the Scriptures speak, we speak; where they are silent, we are silent" might be regarded as categorizing the ethos of the movement.[14]

Partly because of this element in the Adventist heritage, James White experienced considerable difficulty in getting his fellow Adventists to unite in a formal organization.[15] It was not until 1872 that a statement of fundamental beliefs was published, and it was clearly stated in this publication that Adventists had "no articles of faith, creed or discipline aside from the Bible."[16]

These constraints—a sense of eschatological urgency combined with anticreedal and antiformalist sentiments—predisposed thought in the direction of the practical work of the church and was hardly congenial to the consideration of theological issues such as the nature of the church. Adventist thought and practice have largely centered about functional rather than ontological concerns.

As we face the beginning of a new millennium, it seems important that we think again of the purpose for which God called the church into being and take stock of what we are—and should be—doing. But this exercise will be immensely enriched if we start by thinking about what the church is. This takes us back to the Pauline ellipse with its twin foci and to a consideration of the body of Christ imagery.

I cannot recall anything in Adventist sources that would lead us to interpret this body imagery as pointing to the church as an extension of the incarnation of Christ on earth in an ontological sense. This would be out of keeping with the general ethos of our self-understanding. How, then, are we to understand this imagery, and what does it signify for our understanding of the nature of the church?

Quite clearly this is a powerful symbol that signifies the profound relationship between the divine and the human in the church. It is possible to have a high view of the church and recognize the presence of the divine in its midst without going to the lengths of affirming the ontological oneness of the church with Christ. The church has been gathered into one body by the Holy Spirit, whose affirming presence remains in its midst.

The profound symbolism of this image points to an even more profound mystery—that of the presence of Christ in the church. This is a mystery that is not explicable in ordinary categories of human reason. Paul does not attempt to explain the divine presence in the church in metaphysical terms. To do so would amount to reductionism. Writing of the union of Christ with the church, he simply affirms, "This is a great mystery" (Eph. 5:22), and perhaps this is a warning to us not to attempt more. But if there is one thing more than another that we all need in this secular age, it is a sense of the profound mystery that Jesus Christ is present to His followers and to the world in a particular sense in the church. It is here that His affirming and guiding presence are made manifest as in no other place.

We began with Wesley; we close with Ellen White. "Through the church eventually will be made manifest the final and full display of the love of God to the world."[17]

[1] Nehemiah Curnock, ed., *The Journal of the Rev. John Wesley, A.M.,* (Naperville, Ill.: Allenson, 1903), vol. 1, p. 469, note 2.

[2] Robert N. Bellah et al., *Habits of the Heart: Individualism and Commitment in American Life* (Berkeley, Calif.: University of California Press, 1985).

[3] Preface to *Hymns and Sacred Poems* (1739), in Albert C. Outler and Richard P. Heitzenrater, eds., *John Wesley's Sermons: An Anthology* (Nashville: Abingdon, 1991), p. 193.

[4] "Upon Our Lord's Sermon on the Mount," Discourse 4, 1.1, in Albert C. Outler, ed., *The Works of John Wesley,* (Nashville: Abingdon, 1984), vol. I. sermon 1, p. 533.

[5] *Ibid.,* 3.1.

[6] *Ibid.,* 1.2.

[7] *Ibid.,* 1.7.

[8] *Ibid.,* 2.2.

[9] See David Lowes Watson, *The Early Methodist Class Meeting: Its Origins and Significance* (Nashville: Discipleship Resources, 1987).

[10] See Arthur L. White, *Ellen G. White: The Early Years, 1827-1862* (Hagerstown, Md.: Review and Herald Pub. Assn., 1985), pp. 32-44. Her writings contain many references to social meetings.

[11] See Ellen G. White, "Social Meetings," *Testimonies for the Church* (Mountain View, Calif.: Pacific Press Pub. Assn., 1948), vol. 2, pp. 577-582.

[12] *Ibid.,* pp. 578, 579.

[13] Ontology is derived from the Greek word *ontos,* which means "being." It is concerned with the question of essential nature, essence, or being. An ontological relationship is thus one of essential essence rather than of similarity or spiritual affinity .

[14] Thomas Campbell, "Declaration and Address," in H. Shelton Smith et al., eds., *American Christianity: An Historical Interpretation With Representative Documents* (New York: Charles Scribner's Sons, 1960-1963), vol. 1, pp. 578-586.

[15] See R. W. Schwarz, *Light Bearers to the Remnant* (Mountain View, Calif.: Pacific Press Pub. Assn., 1979), pp. 93-98.

[16] In Schwarz, p. 167.

[17] Ellen G. White, *Testimonies to Ministers* (Mountain View, Calif.: Pacific Press Pub. Assn., 1923), p. 50.

CHAPTER 7

In, but Not of, the World

L et your bearing towards one another arise out of your life in Christ Jesus" (Phil. 2:5, NEB). "For many, of whom I have often told you and now tell you even with tears, live as enemies of the cross of Christ. Their end is destruction, their god is the belly, and they glory in their shame, with minds set on earthly things. But our commonwealth is in heaven, and from it we await a Savior, the Lord Jesus Christ, who will change our lowly body to be like his glorious body" (Phil. 3:18-21, RSV).

In this passage the apostle Paul contrasts two very different groups of people. On the one hand are those whose minds are "set on earthly things." On the other are those with a dual citizenship. They live on this earth and of necessity interact with members of the wider society, but all the while they are citizens of a higher realm. Ultimately their citizenship is in heaven. That citizenship defines their relationship with the wider society and constitutes the basis upon which decisions are made regarding life in their earthly citizenship. It provides a horizon of values that facilitates the evaluation of all earthly realities. Such citizens are guided by a higher and constant vision that gives purpose and meaning to life.

One of the classical scriptural representations of the life driven by a heavenly vision is found in the eleventh chapter of the letter to the Hebrews. "These all died in faith, not having received what was promised, but having seen and greeted it from afar, and having acknowledged that they were strangers and exiles on the earth. For people who speak thus make it clear that they are seeking a homeland. If they had been thinking of that land from which they had gone out, they would have had opportunity to return. But as it is, they desire a better country, that is, a heavenly one. Therefore God is not ashamed to be called their God, for he has prepared for them a city" (Heb. 11:13-16, RSV).

Thus far we have applied the passage in Philippians to the pilgrimage of the individual Christian, but it is not possible to think merely of the relationship of the individual to the wider society. Inevitably the community of faith comes into view, and when the issue is thus broadened to that of the relationship of the community of faith to the world, the picture takes on added complexity.

There has been general agreement through the ages that the Christian life is guided by a light from above that gives a sense of purpose and standards of moral judgment. But when it comes to the details of relationships ideally obtaining between Christians and society, there has almost always been a wide variety in both belief and practice.

On the one hand, there have been those who have been acutely aware of the tension between sinful society and the practice of the Christian life. Some, such as hermits, monks, mystics, and members of religious communal societies, have sought to withdraw from the wider society and its distractions. On the other hand, some have regarded the church as standing in a relationship of continuity with morally respectable society and so have experienced little tension regarding the relationship.

In approaching the question of the relationship of the Seventh-day Adventist Christian to the world, let us start from the larger picture of the church in, but not of, the world and then return to the individual.

Two Polar Views
The Church as a Religious Communal Society—There have

been many ideas regarding the ideal relationship of the church to the world. The concept of the church as a religious communal society, which derives from the example of the first Jerusalem church, has remained alive through the centuries. There have been several expressions of this in North America. Among them, George Rapp's Harmony Society, Noyes' Oneida Community, the Amana Colonies, Hutterites, and Mennonite intentional communities.

These communal societies are kept together by the force of a religious vision and indeed are inconceivable without compelling religious constraints. The Hutterites, which have more than 380 communal communities and about 35,000 members in North America, are surely one of the most successful religious communal societies in the annals of the Christian church. Hutterite farming communities are almost totally closed off from the wider society.

Mennonite intentional religious communities, on the other hand, viewed from the outside hardly appear to be communal societies. Members go about their daily lives in the usual kinds of occupations and mingle with members of society quite naturally. Closer inspection, though, reveals a truly communal society in which possessions and responsibilities are shared.

In the modern world it is particularly churches in the Anabaptist "Believer's Church" tradition that have regarded the religious communal society, with a degree of separation from the world, as the ideal form of Christian discipleship. Anabaptists felt the magisterial Reformers had not gone far enough in this direction. The Schleitheim Confession of 1527 defines their view regarding separation from the world and all things evil. "A separation shall be made from the evil and from the wickedness which the devil planted in the world; in this manner, simply that we shall not have fellowship with them. . . . For truly all creatures are in but two classes, good and bad, believing and unbelieving, darkness and light, the world and those who [have come] out of the world.

"To us then the command of the Lord is clear when He calls upon us to be separate from the evil."[1]

Thus at one end of the pattern of relationships between the church and the world are the religious communal societies. The more I learn about some of these, the more beautiful appear the spiritual and interpersonal relationships they engender. Their mutual support and sharing and care for the aged and students and persons in need seems to be a beautiful antidote to so many of the ills of our winner-take-all society. And yet, like countless others, I ask myself whether I could relinquish much of the personal decision-making of my life to the control of the group. Most of us are too much children of this world, too much molded by its influence, to fit into such groups.

The Church as a Theocracy—At the opposite extreme from the communal forms of Christianity and radical separation from the world is the concept of a theocracy. Taking the experience of Israel before the monarchy as an example, John Calvin was convinced that a theocracy in which the church leads in the establishment of the rule of God on the earth was the ideal. The Puritans, having been schooled in this way of thinking at Geneva, endeavored to establish a theocracy in England, and also carried this ideal with them to Massachusetts, where they established a commonwealth in which they sought to realize the ideal of the rule of God in both church and state.

Neither the concept of communal Christianity nor Christian theocracy appears to be a realistic possibility in the contemporary world. Beautiful as is the ideal of the religious communal society, it seems to be functional for only a special kind of religious virtuoso, unless one is born into such a group. And whereas the ideal of a theocracy is conceivable in relatively small face-to-face societies, it is inconceivable to us in the contemporary secular world. We await God's great theocracy in the kingdom to come. There is a range of views, however, between these two poles. These are summarized below as a foil against which to discuss an Adventist understanding of the relationship between the church and the world.

A Triangle of Intermediate Views

John Howard Yoder has presented us with a typology that seems to me to be more helpful than the familiar four-type model of H. R. Niebuhr. These he describes as the **activist** church, the **conversionist** church, and the **confessing** church.[2]

The Activist Church—Activist churches, represented by many of the mainline churches, seek to exert a positive influence upon the wider society in a variety of ways. In addition to programs to spread and transmit the gospel, they decry injustice and inequity and become involved in schemes for the humanization of the social order.

These churches have a tendency to emphasize Christian social ethics and social renewal as much as personal ethics and the proclamation of the gospel. Such churches are thus deeply involved in the affairs of the world, to the extent at times of taking their agenda from the world rather than from the Word of God. Mission may be defined as cooperating with what God is doing in the world rather than seeking for the conversion of souls.

The general criticism is that activist churches lack adequate detachment from the world to enable their members to see the world for what it is.

The Conversionist Church—Conversionist churches stress personal response to God in the experience of conversion. This view of the church is usually coupled with a sense of eschatological urgency and is perhaps the closest to Moody's lifeboat metaphor. Time is late, evil is abundant and widespread, and there is little hope that the involvement of the church in the reengineering of unjust social structures will significantly counter the effects of human sin. Hope of creating an utopia on earth is regarded as a false dream. The only real hope of changing society is personal conversion, repentance of sin, and reconciliation with God. This results in changed persons, whose lives then witness to the way things should be.

Conversionist churches help their members see the world for what it is by providing a vision of what is right and wrong and a sense of history that looks forward to the ultimate triumph of God and the establishment of the kingdom of righteousness. Such churches usually have clearly defined beliefs, standards of behavior, and conditions of membership. They function as primary groups that define a total response to life. Members may be active in the wider society, but spiritual formation within the group inculcates a set of values that are largely at odds with those of the society.

Characteristically, conversionist groups, despite a strong sense of identity and separation from the world, tend to emphasize individual above corporate experience. This may stem in part from a stress on personal conversion, being right with the Lord in the daily life, and concern regarding preparation for the final judgment. Several evangelical thinkers have sought to counter this tendency with an emphasis on corporate experience.[3] Many evangelical congregations and Adventists are closer to the conversionist than to either the activist or confessing church models.

The Confessing Church—Confessing churches are represented by some of the Anabaptist groups, including the Mennonites. Hallmarks of confessing churches are a strong communal impulse and a tendency to reject any utopian humanitarianism. Emphasis is placed on spiritual formation rather than on conversion. Children growing up in the group are engrafted into the church progressively in stages of growth and development rather than in a climactic conversion experience. Issues confronting the church are discussed by the community, and consensual solutions that faithfully reflect the gospel are sought. There is an emphasis on corporate worship and perhaps above all upon the formation of a community of faith that is a witness to the uniting love of God—a community in which persons honor others above themselves, are transparently honest, keep their promises, respect and assist the poor, and are willing to suffer for righteousness. The most powerful witness to the world is regarded first and foremost as being a community that realizes the teachings of the Sermon on the Mount in its daily experience. Confessing communities seek to provide a model of what human society could be rather than trying to reengineer existing social structures.

We have briefly outlined a triad of types in the paragraphs above. No community of faith exactly fits any of these types. However, they provide a foil that serves to highlight the characteristics of particular communities. And this in turn facilitates reflective thought about our own community of faith. In order to clarify our self-perception of the Adventist Church further, four classical functions of the church that serve as useful instruments of analysis are outlined next.

Four Classical Functions of the Church

Four functions of the church derive from the New Testament, and although they do not always receive equal weight, they are generally regarded as descriptive of the major features of the life and work of the church: **witness**—*kerygma and martyria;* **community or fellowship**—*koinōnia;* **service**—*diakonia;* and **worship**—*leitourgia.*

Notable about these functions is that they relate to a community and not simply to an individual or to a loosely aggregated group of people. First, they have to do with the vertical relationship between the community and the divine in worship. Second, they describe the horizontal relationships of fellowship and service within the community. Third, they define functions of service and witness to the wider world.

Witness—God has chosen to fulfill His purposes on earth by calling together a people—as is evidenced in both the Old and New Testaments—to show forth His goodness. The community of faith is not to bottle up the good news and keep it to itself. One of the fundamental reasons for the existence of the church is the fulfillment of the mission of Christ. But the church is not simply the bearer of the message of redemption as a mouthpiece reciting the Word. God called a community into being as a living witness to the power of the gospel.

The primary dimension of the relationship of the church to the world is that of witness. And this can be achieved only when the church faithfully represents the love and teachings of the Master in its daily life. Of course, the message must be widely proclaimed, but this must be given credence by the distinctness of the new community of faith.

Fellowship, Community—The Greek word *koinōnia* means that which is held in common, or sharing. It is used in the New Testament to describe the sharing of both spiritual resources and material possessions. Both kinds of sharing have been common in Christianity through the ages.

In a sense, fellowship in the full depth of its meaning defines relationship with the world in a negative sense, but only partially so. The Christian disciple has a primary relationship with, and derives strength from, the community of faith. This does not necessarily imply total separation from the world, as some have held. Rather, disciples bear witness to the faith in their daily association with unbelievers and in so doing draw interested persons into the fellowship of the community.

Perhaps the greatest threats to community in the Western world are individualism and institutionalism. The isolation of individualism, the "lonely crowd" syndrome, is what makes the social wholeness of the community both so attractive and so difficult for us to achieve. Institutionalism makes it easier for individuals to slough off responsibility for the work of the church and adopt the attitude that "it is their responsibility and not mine." Both attitudes can speed the transition from an active movement to a church maintenance syndrome. True fellowship should result in ministry and mission by the whole people of God.

Ministry of Service—At the heart of the Christian community is a spirit of self-sacrificing service manifested in deeds such as uplifting the downtrodden, honoring the poor, and caring for those who are old and weak. The prime example is the compassionate Jesus, who cared for the needs of many and bound up the brokenhearted during His earthly ministry.

Paul styled himself a "servant of Christ Jesus, . . . set apart for the service of the Gospel" (Rom. 1:1, NEB) and as "every man's servant" (1 Cor. 9:19, NEB) in order to win as many as possible.

The passage most frequently quoted in this connection is: "The kind of religion which is without stain or fault in the sight of God our Father is this: to go to the help of orphans and widows in their distress" (James 1:27, NEB).

Diakonia of this kind was called "disinterested benevolence" by evangelicals in the nineteenth century. By this they indicated that the investment of means and self in others was without trace of self-interest. Ellen White advocated the practice of disinterested benevolence and lamented that it "is very rare in this age of the world."[4]

Diakonia comes to full expression within the community of faith and particularly so in communal societies, but it should certainly not be restricted to the confines of the fellowship. Service rendered in a true spirit of disinterested benevolence, no matter how small the act or service, is one of the instrumentalities that breaks down barriers between the inner community and the outside world.

Worship—Worship might be defined as engagement with the sacred. It is one of the primary tasks of the church, for it is from the central experience of worship and communion with God that strength and vision for the other functions of the church derive. Worship reveals God's heights and goodness and our depths of poverty. It lifts us up, for it is in worship that the love and power of God's work of redemption in Jesus Christ becomes real to us. Commenting on John 4:23: "But the hour is coming, and is now here, when the true worshipers will worship the Father in spirit and truth," William Temple wrote: "Worship is the submission of all our nature to God. It is the quickening of conscience by holiness; the nourishment of mind with His truth; the purifying of imagination by His beauty; the opening of the heart to His love; the surrender of will to His purpose—and all of this gathered up in adoration, the most selfless emotion of which our nature is capable and therefore the chief remedy for that self-centeredness which is our original sin and the source of all actual sin."[5]

Worship involves the sacrifice of our bodies. "I appeal to you therefore . . . , by the mercies of God, to present your bodies as a living sacrifice, holy and acceptable to God, which is your spiritual worship" (Rom. 12:1). This involves the total surrender of our lives to God, including the things we love, prayer and service, forgiveness of one another, and the sharing of our possessions. "Through him, then, let us continually offer a sacrifice of praise to God, that is, the fruit of lips that confess his name. Do not neglect to do good and to share what you have, for such sacrifices are pleasing to God" (Heb. 13:15, 16).

Adventists in, but Not of, the World

In closing, we return to the passages in Philippians with which we opened this chapter. Two categories of persons are contrasted—those with "minds set on earthly things" and those whose "commonwealth [one might say citizenship] is in heaven." As Adventists we neither retreat from the world like hermits, nor seek to build the City of God on earth. We walk the dusty streets of the earthly city and hold communion with its citizens, but at the same time it is with a prayer that the radiance of our faces and the goodness of our ways bear testimony to our higher citizenship. And we seek to tell the message with clarity and in winsome ways.

We are cognizant that the apostle Paul gives special words of admonition to the citizens of the commonwealth: "Let your bearing towards one another arise out of your life in Christ Jesus" (Phil. 1:5, NEB). Perhaps one of our greatest needs is grace to form more accepting and loving communities of faith—communities that are warm and confirming and filled with the joy of our Lord, communities that do even more to aid those who need help and welcome the downcast into their midst, communities that can encourage those who suffer from intangible forms of pain and who need the moral support and uplift that comes from the heart of a caring community.

W. A. Spicer was quite right. The Adventist family is a wonderful family to belong to. The challenge to us is whether we can make it an even more wonderful family—clearer in its witness, stronger in its corporate mutuality, and more deeply spiritual when we come to the throne of worship. God give us grace as we seek to make our communities of faith on this earth signs of that commonwealth in which we hold our true citizenship.

---

[1] The Schleitheim Confession (1527), article 4, in John H. Leith, ed., *Creeds of the Churches,* (Atlanta: John Knox Press, 1982), pp. 285, 286.

[2] See John Howard Yoder, "'A People in the World': Theological Interpretation," in James Leo Garrett, Jr., ed., *The Concept of the Believers' Church* (Scottdale, Pa.: Herald Press, 1969), pp. 250-284.

[3] See for instance, Stanley J. Grenz, *Revisioning Evangelical Theology* (Downers Grove, Ill.: InterVarsity Press, 1993), pp. 148-162.

[4] Ellen G. White, *Testimonies for the Church* (Mountain View, Calif.: Pacific Press Pub. Assn., 1948), vol. 3, p. 516.

[5] William Temple, *Readings in St. John's Gospel* (London: MacMillan and Co., Ltd., 1945), p. 68.

CHAPTER 8

A Holy People

The religion of Christ means more than the forgiveness of sin; it means taking away our sins, and filling the vacuum with the graces of the Holy Spirit. It means divine illumination, rejoicing in God. It means a heart emptied of self, and blessed with the abiding presence of Christ. When Christ reigns in the soul, there is purity, freedom from sin. The glory, the fullness, the completeness of the gospel plan is fulfilled in the life. The acceptance of the Saviour brings a glow of perfect peace, perfect love, perfect assurance. The beauty and fragrance of the character of Christ revealed in the life testifies that God has indeed sent His Son into the world to be its Saviour." [1]

In the Pastoral Epistles (Timothy and Titus) Paul does not write about faith and law and grace as he does in the theological letters to the Galatians and Romans. He deals instead with practical matters relating to the church and Christian life, issues such as godliness and good works and church order.

The substance of this is summed up in Titus 2:14. It is encouraging to note that in this text it is Jesus Christ who redeems us from every "lawless deed" and purifies "His own special people, zealous for good works" (NKJV). The beautiful description by Ellen White of the dynamics of holiness, cited in the first paragraph of this chapter, while not written as a commentary on this text, magnificently explicates its meaning. A life of holiness (she uses the term *completeness*) stemming from the presence of

Christ within the soul should be a wonderful experience and not a legalistic doctrine.

It is hardly popular to speak about holiness these days. We prefer to hear about justification by faith or being clothed with Christ's righteousness. Perhaps this is because we know ourselves and our earthly tendencies too well to think of ourselves as holy. We rejoice in the wonderful deliverance of the salvation that is ours and find it easier to speak of forgiveness than of holiness. We read such passages as "Pursue . . . holiness without which no one will see the Lord" (Heb. 12:14) and "The condition of eternal life is now just what it has always been, . . . perfect obedience to the law of God, perfect righteousness"[2] and ask whether we can live up to such standards, try as we might.

In addition, concentration upon the achievement of holiness may fuel an incentive toward a discouraging legalism and undercut the experience of assurance. And eschatological anxiety, even though mild, adds existential reality to such concerns. On balance, it is more comforting to push such thoughts aside and simply continue on the Christian way, trusting in the goodness of our Lord Jesus Christ. But this is hardly an appropriate response. We are constantly encouraged in both Scripture and the writings of Ellen White to put on the garments of holiness.

Perhaps I have overdrawn the picture of our reluctance regarding holiness, and if so, that is good, because holiness is a natural and beautiful part of the Christian way of salvation. Furthermore, it should be a comforting doctrine that confirms the efficacy of grace and supports the experience of assurance rather than leading to legalism. Why, then, is there an ambivalence on the part of many toward this doctrine?

The thesis of this chapter is that unease regarding holiness is at least partially the result of a centuries-old tendency to fragment the gospel. As is indicated by the theme paragraph above, there is a wonderful wholeness to the gospel. By fragmentation I mean the inclination to concentrate upon one aspect of the way of salvation, such as the forgiveness of sins, to the relative neglect of other dimensions of the whole. The incarnation of

Christ, His work upon the cross, justification by faith, sanctification, the restoration of the image of God in human beings, holiness, resurrection to eternal life, and so on, are all parts of God's wonderful work of salvation. No single aspect by itself does justice to the comprehensive wonder of it all.

The tendency toward fragmentation extends to the relationship between divine sovereignty and human responsibility in the way of salvation. On the one hand, emphasis may be placed one-sidedly upon God's work—i.e., on a doctrine of justification by faith by grace alone, which undercuts the sense of human responsibility. On the other hand, concentration upon human responsibility may result in a joyless legalism.

In the first case, consideration of personal holiness is practically precluded, because salvation is all of grace. It is argued that Christ's righteousness is imputed to us, and therefore we need none of our own. All the responsibility is lodged with God. Grace may thus be distorted into an antinomianism that amounts to a betrayal of the central meaning of the gospel. In the second case, there may be a fear of judgment and a striving for holiness that turns the gospel into a discouraging legalism that amounts to a denial of our Lord's grace.

Both are examples of the tendency to fragment the gospel.

Holiness in the New Testament

Jesus' Teaching—The word "holy" and its cognates is used frequently in the New Testament. However, Jesus commonly uses the word "righteousness" (which comes from a different Greek root) rather than holiness in referring to the attributes of His followers. The Sermon on the Mount is probably the best known and most discussed part of the New Testament. It reveals both the gift and demand of the gospel and is the passage most often referred to in expositions of the teachings of Jesus regarding both holiness and the law.

Jesus' announcement of the kingdom (Matt. 4:23) and His encouragement of the disciples to share His sense of being sons of God provide the background for the sermon. The Lord's

Prayer (Matt. 6:7-15) is the centerpiece of the whole, and the determining clause of the prayer is that the will of God might be done.

The passage that relates most directly to righteousness or holiness is Matthew 5:20-48. It begins "unless your righteousness exceeds that of the scribes and Pharisees, you will never enter the kingdom of heaven" and ends "be perfect, therefore, as your heavenly Father is perfect." In between these verses is a series of six statements with the structure, "You have heard that it was said . . . But I say to you . . ." In each case there is a statement of the demand of the law followed by a statement that raises obedience to a spiritual level.

The purpose of the passage is to teach that the righteousness of the followers of Jesus Christ is not that of obedience to a legal requirement as the Pharisees taught, but a matter of the heart and of inner conformity to God's will. This is in keeping with the Greek word *telos,* translated "perfect" in Jesus' speech. It means whole, mature, and signifies complete goodness; a through-and-through kind of goodness that stems from the heart.

The same point is made in Matthew 6:1-18. This passage immediately follows Jesus' statement of perfection and contains the Lord's Prayer. Here three parallel examples are given of the external righteousness of the Pharisees—almsgiving, fasting, and prayer. The truly righteous do not perform these for outward recognition, as the hypocrites do, but from the heart. Here again, it is purity of motive and not external observance of the ordinance that matters. The sermon points to a righteousness that stems from a heart which is fully conformed to the will of God rather than to a rectitude that consists in compliance with an external moral code.

An important aspect of the discussion as to what Jesus teaches regarding holiness is whether the Sermon on the Mount should be regarded as law or gospel. If it is law, then what precisely is the proper function of this restatement of the law? Some Protestants have tended to separate law from, or oppose it to, gospel. They regard the Sermon on the Mount as law—a magnification of the Decalogue, as Moses quadrupled. The major function of the law, on this view, is to reveal and convict of sin. It demonstrates that the demands of the law cannot be fulfilled and so drives the sinner in penitence to the foot of the cross. There, God in His graciousness grants forgiveness (justification by faith) and covers the soul with Christ's righteousness (imputed righteousness). Law has then fulfilled its task.

But law is not opposed to gospel in the teaching of Jesus; the two are woven together. The message Jesus proclaimed is not that the reign of law of the old dispensation has come to an end, now to be followed by the sweet harmony of the gospel. In His own life He stood on the side of law, and hence was often called a rabbi. He exemplified the righteousness He spoke about. On the other hand, unlike the Pharisees (the name means the separate ones) He did not separate Himself from sinners. He consorted with sinful men and women and was said to be a friend of publicans and sinners.

The words of forgiveness He spoke were also law: "Neither do I condemn thee: go, and sin no more" (John 8:11). And the judgments He spoke were also gospel (Luke 7:47-50). The miracle of the gospel is precisely that law and gospel function together as a regenerating power in the Christian experience. The teaching of Jesus indicates that righteousness (i.e., holiness) stems from a heart that is fully attuned to the divine will, rather than something that is achieved by the fulfillment of an external code.

Paul's Teaching—Holiness and its cognates, as used by Paul and other New Testament authors, appear frequently in the New Testament and in the early Christian writings. It signifies both a state of holiness—"And may he so strengthen your hearts in holiness that you may be blameless" (1 Thess. 3:13)—and the process of making holy, as in Colossians 1:28 and Ephesians 4:13. It is both a condition and a process. The believer lives in holiness and grows into holiness by the grace of God.

It has been common in Protestantism to place so much emphasis on the Pauline doctrine of justification by faith that his remarkable passages on sanctification/holiness have often been overlooked. Both of the sustained admonitions to holiness in the New Testament were written by Paul. The passage in the First Letter to the Thessalonians often styled the locus classicus of holiness is: "May he make your hearts firm, so that you may stand before our God and Father holy and faultless when our Lord Jesus comes with all those who are his own" (1 Thess. 3:13, NEB). Paul adds that it is "the will of God, that you should be holy. . . . For God called us to holiness, not to impurity" (1 Thess. 4:3-7, NEB).

Later yet Paul adds: "For God has not destined us to the terrors of judgment, but to the full attainment of salvation through our Lord Jesus Christ. . . . Be always joyful; pray continually. . . . May God himself, the God of peace, make you holy in every part, and keep you sound in spirit, soul, and body, without fault when our Lord Jesus Christ comes. He who calls you is to be trusted; he will do it" (1 Thess. 5:9, 16, 17, 23, 24, NEB).

The other sustained Pauline discussion is in Romans 6:2, 6, 11, 14, 22.

These passages describe an ongoing process toward holiness rather than what might be called perfected perfection. The believers to whom Paul writes have not yet obtained holiness in its fullness. They are on the way, as are the Christians in Philippi, to whom Paul writes: "The one who began a good work among you will bring it to completion by the day of Jesus Christ" (Phil. 1:6). And in his autobiographical passages Paul freely admits that he has not achieved sanctification in its fullness (Phil. 3:12-15).

Paul also uses the word "perfect" (the same word Jesus used in Matthew 5:48), meaning complete or mature, in Colossians 1:28 and Ephesians 4:13, and he gives it essentially the same meaning he gives to holiness or sanctification. Both words are used in conjunction in the phrase "making holiness perfect" in 2 Corinthians 7:1. The implication is that holiness does not of itself mean a state of absolute holiness but that Christians grow into a fullness of holiness.

A triad of passages in the Epistle to the Hebrews also merits attention. Hebrews 10:10 makes clear that it is God's will that sinners be made holy. In Hebrews 12:10 an analogy is drawn. Like an earthly father God disciplines in a creative work in human lives in order that "we may share his holiness." And finally there is this almost fearful admonition: "Pursue . . . the holiness without which no one will see the Lord" (verse 14).

These biblical references are sufficient to indicate that the way of salvation includes more than the forgiveness of sins. The great truth of the gospel by which the church stands or falls is that God forgives our sins, by faith alone, by grace alone. It is a free gift that we do not deserve and cannot earn. But justification is not the totality of the gospel. An equal if not even greater work of grace is the divine functioning of a power that leads the Christian into a fullness of blessing described as becoming "partakers of the divine nature" (2 Peter 1:4).

Fragmentation of the Gospel[3]

Perhaps the central example of fragmentation in Protestantism is the concentration that took place upon justification by faith. In his reaction against a Catholic penitential system Luther made justification by faith the determining principle of the gospel. An extreme Augustinian doctrine of total depravity—human inability to make any overture in the direction of salvation—is the foil for affirmation of divine sovereignty in salvation. Justification is God's work. Human freedom and responsibility are precluded. The lifelong status of the believer is described in the phrase *simul justus et peccator*—at the same time justified and a sinner. As a result of this emphasis, the gospel is all but limited to the atoning work of Christ.

As an illustration of this tendency consider question 29 of the Westminster Shorter Catechism: "How are we made partakers of the redemption purchased by Christ? Answer. We are made partakers of the redemption purchased by Christ by the effectual application of it to us by His Holy Spirit."[4]

Here the gospel is something that can be called an "it." On the one hand, in this confession the gospel is firmly grounded in the work of Christ on the cross. On the other hand, the relationship of the believer in this experience is described in impersonal terms. An implication of this is that the gospel may be conceived of in doctrinal or propositional terms and salvation as the appropriation of the benefits of Christ rather than in terms of personal communion with a living Saviour, as in the beautiful theme paragraph at the beginning of this chapter.

Largely as a result of the above concentration upon the work of Christ, law came to be separated from gospel. The Reformers strove to define the relationship between law and gospel. But even though they succeeded in defining three distinct uses of the law—the second, and most important, being the function of revealing and convicting of sin—they were not able to resolve what they regarded as the contradiction between law and gospel. Instead of reconciling the tension, they sharply opposed law to gospel. They sought a solution in an alternation between the two. Law functioned *outside, before,* and *after,* but never *with* the gospel.

But if we can overcome this one-sidedness and recover the wholeness of the gospel, which joins Christ's work of atonement with the sanctifying presence of the indwelling Holy Spirit, then holiness becomes a natural expression of the Christian life.

Some More Ellen White References
Note the optimism in Ellen White's writings about the transforming power of grace and the joy of holiness. Consider the following quotations from *Steps to Christ.*

"He who was one with God has linked Himself with the children of men by ties that are never to be broken. . . . He is our Sacrifice, our Advocate, our Brother, bearing our human form before the Father's throne, and through eternal ages one with the race He has redeemed—the Son of man. And all this that man might be uplifted from the ruin and degradation of sin that he might reflect the love of God and share the joy of holiness.

"The price paid for our redemption . . . should give us exalted conceptions of what we may become through Christ.

. . . What a value this places upon man! . . . By assuming human nature, Christ elevates humanity. Fallen men are placed where, through connection with Christ, they may indeed become worthy of the name 'sons of God.'"[5]

"It is impossible for us, of ourselves, to escape from the pit of sin in which we are sunken. Our hearts are evil, and we cannot change them. . . . There must be a power working from within, a new life from above, before men can be changed from sin to holiness. That power is Christ. His grace alone can quicken the lifeless faculties of the soul, and attract it to God, to holiness."[6]

"The 'Light which lighteth every man that cometh into the world' illumines the secret chambers of the soul, and the hidden things of darkness are made manifest. Conviction takes hold upon the mind and heart. The sinner has a sense of the righteousness of Jehovah and feels the terror of appearing, in his own guilt and uncleanness, before the Searcher of hearts. He sees the love of God, the beauty of holiness, the joy of purity; he longs to be cleansed and to be restored to communion with Heaven."[7]

"A life in Christ is a life of restfulness. There may be no ecstasy of feeling, but there should be an abiding, peaceful trust. Your hope is not in yourself; it is in Christ. . . . It is by loving Him, copying Him, depending wholly on Him, that you are to be transformed into His likeness.

"Jesus says, 'Abide in Me.' These words convey the idea of rest, stability, confidence."[8]

"He has granted men the privilege of becoming partakers of the divine nature, and, in their turn, of diffusing blessings to their fellow men. This is the highest honor, the greatest joy, that it is possible for God to bestow upon men."[9]

There is much that is striking in these passages. Perhaps the first thing to notice is the bright picture portrayed regarding human nature. Having taken our human nature, Christ continues to bear it in some sense before the Father's throne. And in assuming our nature "Christ elevates humanity." This should serve to "give us exalted conceptions of what we may become through Christ" and open our eyes to see the great "value this places upon man."

Second, one of the most frequently quoted biblical texts in her writings contains the beautiful clause "come to share in the very being of God" (2 Peter 1:4, NEB). She describes this in several ways: as the creation of a new being in the image of God, being clothed with the righteousness of Christ, and so on. Holiness is a healing of the corruption of one's nature.

Third, she frequently writes of holiness as being "restored to communion with Heaven" and "to be restored to harmony and communion with God."[10] Salvation is not some impersonal "it" applied to the soul; it is grounded in a relationship with the divine.

Fourth, Ellen White does not oppose law to gospel. As in the life and teachings of Jesus, law is a part of the gospel. But holiness is not achieved by compliance with law. Holiness stems from within—from harmony with the will of God.

Fifth, she frequently writes of the "joy of holiness." These and other passages give one the feeling that the disciple seriously following Jesus has entered a state of joyous freedom and happiness.

Sixth, the joy of holiness is coupled with a reciprocal sense of the love of God. The implication is that holiness is not achieved by a pilgrimage of drudgery in which every earthly inclination is laboriously cut off. Holiness grows from perfect love for, and personal communion with, God.

Seventh, holiness is brought about by a Power working from above, which generates new desires and purposes. This is as much a function of grace as is forgiveness or justification.

Finally, Ellen White is an apostle of both holiness and assurance. The true Christian life ushers in a state of restfulness—"an abiding, peaceful trust." Holiness, as she describes the experience, does not drag the Christian back into legalism, and neither does it undercut assurance. It finds expression in a life of joyous discipleship.

Ellen White here presents an optimistic and inspiring picture of the Christian pilgrimage, which is somewhat at odds with that of classical Protestantism with its pessimistic doctrine of human depravity, rather one-sided emphasis upon a high solifidian doctrine of justification, easy acceptance of the doctrine that the Christian always remains both justified and a sinner, and near neglect of growth in the process of sanctification.

Holiness, then, is not a legalistic doctrine. It is a natural result of the power of the gospel working in the soul. With the recovery of the wholeness of the gospel, as expressed in the writings of Ellen White, the legalistic and discouraging tendencies inherent in some concepts of holiness disappear. May this be our personal experience as we look forward to the day of union with the heavenly host.

---

[1] Ellen G. White, *Christ's Object Lessons* (Mountain View, Calif.: Pacific Press Pub. Assn., 1900), pp. 419, 420.

[2] _____, *Steps to Christ* (Mountain View, Calif.: Pacific Press Pub. Assn., 1956), p. 62.

[3] I am indebted to Prof. G. Hendry, one of my theological mentors in graduate school, for introducing me to concepts of the fragmentation and impersonalization of the gospel, which I briefly adumbrate in this chapter. His concern for a wholeness that holds both law and gospel and the person and work of Christ together in the way of salvation made an indelible impression on my consciousness, because so much of it parallels the Adventist/Ellen White understanding of the way of salvation. He introduced me to his study, *The Gospel of the Incarnation* (Philadelphia: The Westminster Press, 1958), in which he seeks to counter the narrowness of the doctrine of salvation of the Western church.

[4] *The Shorter Catechism of the Westminster Assembly* (Philadelphia: Presbyterian Board of Publications), p. 20.

[5] E. G. White, *Steps to Christ,* pp. 14, 15.

[6] *Ibid.,* p. 18.

[7] *Ibid.,* p. 24.

[8] *Ibid.,* pp. 70, 71.

[9] *Ibid.,* p. 79.

[10] *Ibid.,* pp. 24, 25.

CHAPTER 9

Salt and Light– Radical Discipleship

In one way or another every chapter in this book deals with the mission of the church. In some we've taken an introspective look at life and fellowship within the community; in others we've turned our gaze outward at the task that is to be done. This chapter is the most overtly outward-looking of all. Every text here referred to, starting with the images of salt and light of the Sermon on the Mount, has to do with some aspect of the mission of the church.

In this chapter we seek to connect Christian experience within the community of faith and the external mission of the church. The two cannot be separated. The going out depends upon the strength within, and the message can have little convincing power if it is not manifested in the experience of the community.

The mission of the church has been fulfilled throughout history in two major ways. There is first the attracting-in dimension of mission, which is more explicitly prominent in the Old than in the New Testament. The community of faith draws others into its midst because of the warmth of its fellowship and spiritually fulfilling worship. And second, there is mission in the more usual sense of going out to others.

The emphasis in the Old Testament is upon Israel's attracting other nations to Jerusalem, whereas the mandate to go out is emphasized in the New Testament. Mission in its comprehensive sense consists of both attracting in and going out. We will pay attention to both, starting with the Messianic prophecies of the later prophets.

Mission as Attracting In

The psalms and later prophets make frequent reference to the Messianic march of the nations to Jerusalem in response to the blessings and acts of God in Israel (see Isa. 2:2-5; 55:5; 60:1-17; Ps. 67; 86:9; 87; and 96:3, 10). The eschatological expectation of the salvation of Israel, prominent in these passages, is also an expectation of salvation for the nations. This is evident in the themes presented in the following passages: "Salvation shall reach the coast lands"; "All peoples shall see the light of the Servant of the Lord"; and "The ends of the earth are called to turn to the Lord" (Isa. 49:6; 42:1-7; 45:22, 23).

A passage that has been significant in Adventist history, both as regards the Sabbath and missions, is practically a summary of the above. "And the foreigners who join themselves to the Lord . . . to be his servants, all who keep the sabbath, and do not profane it, and hold fast my covenant—these I will bring to my holy mountain, and make them joyful in my house of prayer; . . . for my house shall be called a house of prayer for all peoples" (Isa. 56:6, 7).

These prophecies and psalms were read and sung in the worship services in Jerusalem. I like trying to picture the postexilic Jews singing the psalm of the nations (Ps. 67), which is explicit regarding the centripetal role of Israel, and wonder how they felt. Was it as easy for them to pray that all nations might be drawn to God's saving power manifest in Jerusalem as it was to pray that God would bless and cause His face to shine upon them? And what about us? Are we as zealous in our prayers for those who have not yet heard or for those who are no longer Christians as we are about our own needs?

What we do know is that the Jews of the Diaspora, scattered about the Mediterranean world during the intertestamental period (see Acts 2:5-11), succeeded·in attracting many proselytes into their midst. Apparently they later became enthusiastically evangelistic and went out to gather the Gentiles into their midst. Jesus recognized their missionary zeal when He commented: "You travel over sea and land to win one convert" (Matt. 23:15, NEB). His negative statement about the lawyers and the Pharisees in this context should not be understood as a condemnation of their missionary zeal. It was a rebuke of the distorted legalism they imposed upon new believers.

What was it about the Jewish communities that made them so attractive to the Gentiles?

First, the Jews themselves had changed. The consciousness that they were a people defined by a Messianic hope was fostered by the breakdown of the Jewish nation. As a result, they gained an attitude of openness to their neighbors who were not now their political enemies as had formerly been the case. Perhaps the use of the psalms and later prophets in their worship services had exerted an influence in this respect.

Second, there was much that was attractive about the belief and worship and social cohesion of the Jewish communities. The Hebrew theistic monotheism, which combined a high view of God as transcendent and all-powerful and yet as exercising loving care over His followers, was certainly attractive to the Eastern mind. We use the word "theism" as if it is an abstract theological idea, and tend to lose sight of the ineffable beauty of the understanding of God it portrays. Theism describes a God who is both omnipotent and loving, far and close—a God who rules the universe and yet is active in the affairs of human lives. Christians should never lose sight of the beauty and attractiveness of the theistic God of the Scriptures.

The lesser theisms, as it were, of the great monistic religions of the East are evidence of the attractiveness of theistic deities. It is not enough to have a great overarching philosophical system that accounts for the operations of reality. There is always the longing for a deity who cares, who is approachable, and who can intervene on behalf of the supplicant. Thus there are countless gods and deities upon whom persons can call in these religions. In all probability it was the reverential theism expressed in the worship of the great God of the Old Testament and the experience of this God in practical life that constituted the greatest attraction of the Jewish religion.

Third, the high moral values that are a natural outcome of this theism and that were both taught and maintained in the life of the community were superior to those practiced in the surrounding religions.

Fourth, the caring social solidarity that afforded support to every member of the community, which has almost always been a characteristic of Jewish communities, attracted proselytes into Judaism.

It is clear that Judaism made many proselytes, and while at the outset this was largely accomplished in the manner read about in the psalms and prophets (of attracting persons into the community), later the Jews became aggressively evangelistic and took their Messianic message to the peoples about them.

There is both continuity and discontinuity in the transition from Israel and its witness to the Christian church. God's purpose remains the same. Israel was elected as God's chosen people not so much because of who they were, or for their own salvation, but to be instrumental in the fulfillment of God's purposes for the nations. Their election was an election to service. Mission in the Old Testament was largely, but not exclusively, centripetal. The Christian church, as we have noted, was called into being to fulfill the purpose of God that Israel had failed to accomplish.

Having fulfilled the covenant with Israel, Christ, who had been seated at the right hand of God and installed as the ruler of the universe, gave the disciples the gospel commission with its four great *"alls."* The first, *"all* authority has been given me," is the foundation of the other three. There follow: *"all* nations," *"all* that I have told you," and *"all* the days." In more specific terms Christ instructed His disciples to bear witness in "Jerusalem, in all Judea and Samaria, and to the ends of the earth" (Acts 1:8).

Missionary outreach in the New Testament was decidedly more centrifugal than it had been in Old Testament days. The disciples went out, and the gospel was preached to much of the then-known world (Rom. 15:20-23; 16:26). However, it would be a mistake to think that their witness was exclusively "going out." Both patterns worked together. As soon as Christian communities were established, they attracted others into their midst—and in many ways this was, and remains, the more radical and compelling of the two forms of witness.

The church is called to witness to our Lord's love and goodness. The Christian message of forgiveness and acceptance, mediated through the preaching of the Word and the celebration of the Lord's Supper, brings great comfort to members. The church is a community in which people love and forgive one another and in which all praise God and rejoice in His goodness. Without this inner experiential witness to the reality of the gospel and the power of forgiveness, the gospel of pardon and acceptance will make little impression on those outside.

Stanley Hauerwas and William Willimon seem at times to be deliberately provocative, and yet there is a fundamental truth in the following: "The most creative social strategy we have to offer is the church. Here we show the world a manner of life the world can never achieve through social coercion or governmental action. We serve the world by showing it something that it is not, namely, a place where God is forming a family out of strangers."*

A Lesson From Peter

I wish to use the first letter of the apostle Peter to elucidate this dual aspect of mission. The letter of Peter is interesting for many reasons. We referred in chapter 8 to the tendency to fragment the gospel. One aspect of this tendency is grounded in a somewhat one-sided reading of the apostle Paul on matters relating to law and grace, justification and atonement, and faith and works. Paul writes little about the life and teaching of Jesus.

Peter, who might be called the other great apostle of the

early church, provides a more balanced portrayal, which covers the teachings of Jesus, the example of His life, and an interpretation of the meaning of His death and resurrection. Perhaps these differences are a consequence of their different experiences. Peter lived with Christ as a disciple, whereas Paul was called to an apostleship out of due season. Paul writes about the great magisterial doctrine of justification by faith (of course, not exclusively), whereas Peter portrays the Christian experience as a lifelong process of growth in faithfulness.

Peter uses the metaphors of a journey (1 Peter 2:21-25), of following in Jesus' footsteps (verse 21), and of being "built into a spiritual house" (verse 5), all of which are indicative of discipleship as a process. Perhaps because of the dominance of Pauline thought in Protestantism, the letter of Peter has not been given adequate weight in the understanding of the way of salvation.

Of more immediate interest to us in this chapter are the twin goals for which the letter seems to have been written. The first is Peter's concern regarding the sense of identity and cohesiveness of the Christian communities in Asia Minor. The second has to do with the mandate of mission and the kinds of life and witness that will make a favorable impression on members of the wider society. The whole is couched in the conviction that the last days are at hand. In fact, the eschatological tone of the Epistle, which is sustained from beginning to end, is without parallel in the New Testament except, perhaps, for the book of Revelation.

Our focus of attention in this chapter on mission is on 1 Peter 2:4-10, where the metaphor is developed of Jesus as the cornerstone of a spiritual temple into which the members, as living stones, are being incorporated. The passage culminates in verses 9 and 10, in which four attributes of Israel are applied to the Gentile Christian communities in Asia Minor and brought to culminating force in a powerful statement of God's purpose for the church. Let us see who these people were before we conduct an exegesis of this passage.

Verse 9 begins with a statement of contrast: "But you . . ."

Some had failed to accept Christ as the cornerstone of the spiritual temple and consequently found in Him a rock of offense upon which they had stumbled. "But you . . ." have accepted Christ and as living stones are being built into a spiritual temple. But the passage seems to imply more than this. It is as if Peter is saying to them, "But you, who are you?" and then points to the enormous contrast between the immense dignity of who they are in Christ and who they appear to be in practical reality. Who are these people then?

They are an exiled persecuted people dispersed among the Gentiles of the five provinces of Asia Minor (1 Peter 1:1). They suffer trials of many kinds, which leads Peter to write that the genuineness of their faith is "tested by fire" (verse 7). Their present circumstances are described as the "time of your exile" (verse 17) and their status as "aliens and exiles" (1 Peter 2:11). Their troubles are a "fiery ordeal" (1 Peter 4:12). Peter addresses these scattered suffering Christians in sublime terms: "Chosen . . . by God the Father . . . sanctified by the Spirit . . . to be sprinkled with his blood" (1 Peter 1:2).

After describing their trials and encouraging them with the assurance of "an inheritance that is imperishable, undefiled, and unfading" (verse 4), Peter describes their faith. "Although you have not seen him, you love him; and even though you do not see him now, you believe in him and rejoice with an indescribable and glorious joy, for you are receiving the outcome of your faith, the salvation of your souls" (verses 8, 9).

This is a picture of surpassing beauty. When we think of Peter we visualize scenes of his discipleship—experiences that revealed the divine beauty of Christ as well as human weakness, yet also of Peter's dramatic and wonderful apostleship. Peter knew and loved the Lord. These scattered Gentile Christians had not seen Christ as had Peter, yet their lives had been touched by His and changed. They loved Him. And in the midst of trials this trust and love enabled them to "rejoice with an indescribable and glorious joy."

Peter, then, in a startling if not provocative manner, ascribes four of the attributes of Israel to these scattered persecuted people: "But you are a chosen race, a royal priesthood, a holy nation, God's own people, in order that you may proclaim the mighty acts of him who called you out of darkness into his marvelous light" (1 Peter 2:9).

"But You Are a Chosen Race [genos]"—The allusion to Israel is inescapable, but what was literally true of Israel was not literally true of these early Christians. Israel was of a common stock—*genos* implies a blood relationship. On the other hand, these Christians were Gentiles and of many races. Only in the blood of Jesus were they one. And in this case the reality portrayed figuratively is more striking than the natural case.

Considerable surprise must have attended the reading of this passage. The force of the passage is heightened by the fact that this is the only use of the word *genos* for Christians in the New Testament. The Christian church is a gathering of people from every race and nation, who have been made one in the blood of Jesus Christ.

"You Are a Royal Priesthood"—This likewise must have greatly surprised those first readers. They were so far removed from any significant social status that one wonders whether they could get past the word "royal" to the concept of priesthood. Peter was letting them know that they were a priesthood that belonged to God and therefore they should reflect His glory. The functions of their priesthood are described: "to offer spiritual sacrifices acceptable to God through Jesus Christ" (verse 5).

Both the above phrases—"chosen race" and "royal priesthood"—are drawn from Exodus 19:5, 6, in which Israel is described as a kingdom of priests. The reference is not to a special class of priests but to the functions of all believers.

These words of Peter lie at the base of the Protestant doctrine of the priesthood of all believers. We are not told explicitly what the functions of this priesthood are, but they doubtless include offering their bodies if need be, giving gifts, singing praises to God, praising God in corporate worship, and witnessing to the wider community by their lives and proclamation.

There are frequent references to the latter in this letter.

"You Are a Holy Nation [ethnos]"—It is highly unusual to use "holy" to modify *ethnos,* the term usually used for Gentiles. This practically amounts to a contradiction in terms. Holy is an attribute of the people of God, *laos,* not of the Gentile nations, *ethnos.* As far as I have been able to determine, this is the only such use in the New Testament. Peter apparently is being deliberately provocative, and his words must have been as striking to the readers as the preceding two attributes.

There is a twofold message here. First, the Gentiles, unholy in themselves, have been reclaimed from their evil ways and sanctified in coming to Christ—the human impossibility has become a reality in Jesus Christ. Second, this is a clear indication that the Christian church—consisting of both Jew and Gentile—has assumed the place of Israel in God's purpose.

"You Are God's Own People [laos]"—Here a third term for people, *laos,* is employed, which in contradistinction to *ethnos* signifies the people of God. God has made these scattered, persecuted Gentile believers His own people. An impossible possibility has taken place. Jew and Gentile have been made one people of God.

These four designations taken together ascribe an astounding dignity and status to these Gentile Christians, a rank that seems to be entirely out of keeping with their social standing and the circumstances of their lives. I find myself wondering at the faith it must have taken for them to recognize themselves, and the purposes of God through them, as they read this passage.

"In Order That You May Proclaim the Mighty Acts of Him Who Called You"—After having ascribed these four sublime attributes to them, Peter completes the sentence with a powerful statement of purpose. They have been called and sanctified and made the people of God *in order that* they might proclaim ("shew forth," as the King James Version interprets the phrase) the praises and mighty acts of God in Jesus Christ.

The church has not been called into existence for its own sake. It has often succumbed to the temptation to celebrate its joy in Christ in sequestered isolation and to rejoice in the company of like-minded saints, in a manner that is more inclined to hide than to proclaim the gospel. But here we are reminded that even though the church may be in straitened circumstances and social disfavor, it has a mandate to fulfill. And the mandate is not given to the leaders of the church only. Here we have the basic teaching regarding the priesthood of all believers—each member is called to offer spiritual sacrifices and proclaim the wonders of our redeeming God.

But how could they, with their limitations and under such difficult circumstances, fulfill this task? It is hardly likely that they could conduct public meetings—they were driven underground by persecution. In addition, Christianity was an illicit religion, without legal standing, in the Roman Empire. How, then, did they witness?

Peter repeatedly encouraged them to live and endure suffering—even as Christ suffered—in such a manner that even those enemies who maligned them would recognize their honorable deeds and come to glorify God. Furthermore, there are several references to mutual love and support within the Christian communities in this letter, which clearly uphold the goal of a very beautiful pattern of relationships and a high level of social solidarity. In addition, there is specific admonition that Christians should "always be ready to make your defense to anyone who demands from you an accounting for the hope that is in you; yet do it with gentleness and reverence" (1 Peter 3:15, 16).

In due course Christianity issued forth to supersede the Caesars. However, there was no evidence these Christians could see that indicated that this was happening. But it did happen precisely because Christians like these in every place both by their lives and their teaching bore witness to the transforming power of grace. The kind of lives they lived in times of persecution, the moral values they upheld, the love and mutual support within the community, the beauty of their devotions and worship, and the power of the answers they gave attracted people into their midst—even notable persons among them. In more hospitable times—when persecution and suppression were relaxed—they could more openly propagate the gospel.

In closing let us briefly consider a few other significant texts.

In 2 Corinthians 4:6 Paul paints a glorious picture that compares the light of Christ shining in the heart of the believer to that first day of Creation, in which God commanded and light broke forth upon the world. The light of "the glory of God in the face of Jesus Christ" is both the basis and motivating force of the mission of the church. I like to picture the Gentile Christians to whom Peter wrote as having the light of life beaming from their faces, regardless of the straitened circumstances of their lives.

Also our Lord said, "I am the light of the world. Whoever follows me will never walk in darkness but will have the light of life" (John 8:12). It is this light that should make the life of every Christian and every Christian community "the light of the world" (Matt. 5:14). It was this light that gave boldness to Peter and John, and it turned the Peter of the denial into the resolute apostle of Pentecost. And so it should also be in the life of every disciple of the Master in this contemporary age.

---

[*]Stanley Hauerwas and William Willimon, *Resident Aliens: A Provocative Christian Assessment of Church and Ministry for People Who Know That Something Is Wrong* (Nashville: Abingdon, 1989), p. 83.

CHAPTER 10

The Adventist Family Today

It would be difficult, if not impossible, to exaggerate the importance of the concern addressed in this chapter. The Adventist family in the United States is in crisis. The family is the building block of the congregation as well as of the church and of society at large, and if the family and the church fail to inspire their young people with the glory of the gospel and the greatness and goodness of God, how can the church fulfill its mission? It will have failed in the most crucial dimension of its task.

The Family in Scripture

That children should be instructed regarding the heritage of Israel and raised in the "fear of the Lord" pervades the Old Testament. When the children of Israel had crossed the river Jordan, Joshua had 12 men, one from each tribe, erect a monument of 12 great stones so that "in days to come, when your children ask what these stones mean" (Joshua 4:6, 7, NEB) they could be told how God had stopped the flow of water and led their ancestors across.

Other memorials, some material and some ritual, such as the annual Passover meal, served to preserve and transmit the heritage from one generation to the next. Prominent among these were the seven annual festivals, three of which required all adult males (including teenage young men) to appear before the Lord at Jerusalem. It is interesting that three of the most important events in the life of our Lord took place at these rituals—initiation into Jewish adulthood at the age of 12 (Luke 2:41-52), His death, and His resurrection. These pilgrimages, the gathering of men from the four corners of Israel, and the other festivals must have made an indelible impression on the young men who participated.

The clearest instructions regarding family relationships in the New Testament are given in Ephesians 5 and 6. Children are to obey and honor parents and show loyalty to them (Eph. 6:1-3; cf. 1 Tim. 5:4). Fathers are instructed: "Do not provoke your children to anger, but bring them up in the discipline and instruction of the Lord" (Eph. 6:4; cf. Col. 3:18-21 and 1 Tim. 5:4). Ephesians 5:21-23 beautifully describes the mutuality and depth of relationships between husbands and wives.

The kind of relationship expected in Christian families is also revealed in the Pastoral Epistles to Timothy and Titus. Church leaders should control their families wisely and well (1 Tim. 3:4, 5, 10-12; Titus 1:5, 6). Widows should assist the younger women to be "loving wives and mothers" (Titus 2:4, 5, NEB).

Additionally, Scripture gives many examples of the influence of godly parents, especially of mothers, upon their children. And Ellen White holds up the example of several of these in her writings on the family.

The Scriptures depict a pattern of order in the family. It offers regulations regarding whom one might and might not marry or divorce, recommendations regarding proper relations between husbands and wives and between parents and children, and the transmission of property.

It is clear from the testimony of Scripture that the family occupied a prominent place in both Israel and the Christian church in transmitting the heritage of belief and in socializing the young and preparing them for the responsibilities of the religious community and of society at large.

As I see it, a most important passage regarding the family is: "Unless the Lord builds the house, those who build it labor in vain. Unless the Lord guards the city, the guard keeps watch in vain. . . . Sons are indeed a heritage from the Lord, the fruit of the womb a reward. Like arrows in the hand of a warrior are the sons of one's youth. Happy is the man who has his quiver full of them. He shall not be put to shame when he speaks with his enemies in the gate" (Ps. 127).

The Hebrew word translated "house" may be interpreted to mean family or household. This psalm describes the ideal family with many faithful sons who will provide security and protection for their parents. And the fundamental lesson is that it is the Lord who builds such a family. There is no real foundation for this kind of faithfulness to family and society apart from belief and trust in the Lord and knowledge of what is right and wrong in His sight. Truly this psalm offers a timeless truth; it defines the foundation of the Christian household.

There is a passage of Scripture that I would add. Apparently even in Israel every family did not turn out as well as is portrayed in Psalm 127. Malachi, the last canonical book of the Old Testament, concludes with a striking message regarding the family. It is clear from the context that God was not pleased with Israel. Worship at the Temple services had fallen into disorder, and there was concern regarding intermarriage with foreign women, which probably led to tension within some families.

The book ends on an eschatological note. The Lord is about to send the prophet Elijah, who will purify and reunite Israel "before the great and terrible day of the Lord comes. He will turn the hearts of parents to their children and the hearts of children to their parents, so that I will not come and strike the land with a curse" (Mal. 4:5, 6).

This is the closing message of the Old Testament. Restoration of the family in the unity of the faith—turning the hearts of parents to their children and vice versa—is a pivotal part of the revival of Israel. Nothing is said here about turning the hearts of parents to each other, but this would seem to be included by the logic of the situation.

The history of the human race in the Hebrew Bible begins

with a marriage and the instruction to be fruitful and multiply. Throughout its pages it provides many examples of the function of the family in maintaining the heritage of and order in Israel. And it closes with a prophetic call that points to the reformation of the family as a central element in the revival of the nation.

Relationships within the family are elevated to a high spiritual level in the Christian Scriptures in a manner that is symbolized by the relationship between Christ and His people and that points forward to that great day on which the families of God on earth are caught up into the unity of the family in heaven.

Status of the Adventist Family

We move from Scripture to the present and the future. What is the present status of the Adventist family in the United States?[1] Twenty years ago professors Charles C. Crider and Robert C. Kistler conducted an extensive study of the Adventist family in America. Their study serves to warn us of far-reaching changes that are taking place. Two of their summary remarks follow.

"This research indicates that the Adventist home is under stress in the United States and enough family units are faltering to pose a crisis for the church as a whole. The church needs to respond affirmatively and forcefully to meet the need, for it is made up of families that comprise its membership."[2]

"In summary one might say that the qualities and characteristics of Adventist families in the United States generally conform to the pattern of other family units in American society. In basic areas where the church holds a specific view which varies from society's norms, about a third to a half of Adventist families have tended to make accommodations which move them away from the teachings of their denomination and closer to the mainstream of contemporary American life. This is especially noted in areas such as the practice of holding daily family worship. In the choice of contemporary music and art forms, recreational activity, vacation patterns, and attitudes toward material possessions, Adventists do not differ greatly from the average American family."[3]

To those who are deeply committed to the church and its mission and who are even remotely aware of the trends in American family life—and general concern in the nation has risen to such a pitch and we are so bombarded with calls of concern from many sources that no one can fail to be at least partially informed—the conclusions of the Crider/Kistler study must be deeply disturbing. If the situation constituted a crisis for the church 20 years ago, how much greater must be the concern now that we are confronted with the continuing development of the trends they describe?

On the brighter side Crider and Kistler found that "differences between Adventist family units and contemporary society are particularly significant in such matters as dating and mating patterns, views on sex and the nature of the marriage bond, divorce, patterns of family organization, and religiosity as expressed in the number of religious things done to confirm adherence to the faith."[4]

The results of the extensive Valuegenesis study[5] conducted at the beginning of this decade confirm the findings of the earlier Crider/Kistler study. The Valuegenesis study was conducted to gain a portrait of academy-age Adventist young people and their attitudes toward home, school, and church. The authors of the report emphasize the positive. However, even so they write: "In spite of the problems and challenges, in spite of the difficult—even perilous—position in which the church finds itself concerning the retention and dedication of the new generation, a silver lining shines through."[6]

Fortunately there is a silver lining, but the cloud itself is dark and foreboding—"even perilous." Adventist young people are almost twice as likely to emphasize the importance of religious faith as are those in mainline churches,[7] and 72 percent thought they would still be active in the Adventist Church at age 40.[8]

It is not surprising that there are chapters in the Valuegenesis report with the titles "Warning! Danger Ahead!" and "A Generation at Risk." And of course a generation at risk means that the church is at risk. The overall impression one receives upon reading the Valuegenesis report is not that of the transmission by church and family and school of a vibrant joyous religion to Adventist young people or that of a church that stimulates their thinking or inspires them with the vision of a great worldwide mission that claims their discipleship or of the maintenance of a high standard of Christian personal and social ethics. And more directly to the point of this chapter, neither is there evidence of the maintenance of fulfilling family devotions in many Adventist homes.

How can the contemporary family best address these issues? As Crider and Kistler point out in the quotations previously cited, despite their semi-isolation and strong sense of identity, Adventists are not immune from the changes taking place in society as a whole. Some of the literature I see on the family seems to advocate a return to the shape of the family at the turn of the century. This would hardly seem to be a viable option, except in isolated cases. The majority of Adventists, of necessity, earn a living and make their contribution to society in the urban setting—and the Adventist upward mobility syndrome is a factor in this. Parents are faced with the challenge of supporting and guiding a family under circumstances in which they are subject to economic pressures, disruptive timetables, intrusive media, a secular social ambience, and crowded schedules for each member of the family.

Increasingly, economic pressures drive wives to work, and conflicting timetables make it difficult for families to find time for worthwhile intellectual discussion and mutual spiritual enrichment. And there is no real possibility of turning the clock back on all of this. Obviously new kinds of solutions must be sought, which may require some hard decisions on the part of some families in the light of what is of ultimate value to them.

Three Problem Areas

Several of the problem areas revealed by the Valuegenesis report seem to be relevant to our present discussion, namely, the declining emphasis on family worship, the difficulty Adventist young people experience with church standards and the tension they feel between standards taught and maintained at home and those taught and enforced by church and school, and the less than inspiring and satisfying church experience of Adventist young people.

Family Devotions—A 1940 survey of 2,000 Adventist young people revealed that only 42 percent reported any kind of family worship in their homes. The Crider and Kistler study found that regular worship was conducted in only 34 percent of Adventist homes.[9] And the Valuegenesis study indicates that daily worship was conducted in fewer than one fourth of Adventist homes.[10] There has obviously been a decline in the practice of united family worship throughout the years. It would appear that the practice has been the victim of default rather than of purposeful neglect. An incipient secularism and the business and complexity of contemporary urban life have much to do with the change. Many families simply give up the attempt and concentrate upon opening and closing Sabbath with worship.

Crider and Kistler list the following reasons for the decline in family worship: the impossibility of finding a time when the family can be together; some family members sleep late while others leave early ("the struggle to force or coerce each one of the children to be present or to participate is too much trouble"); interruptions of all kinds—many related to work or play and travel schedules—are too disruptive; worship interferes with favorite TV programs, and so on.[11] It is difficult in many homes to get the family together for a meal, let alone a worship session.

There is obviously no simple solution, applicable in all cases, to this problem. It constitutes a challenge to each family. Primary responsibility for the formation of character and the transmission of the faith and a sense of living before God in a moral universe lies with the family and cannot be simply abdicated and entrusted to church and school. Ellen White has written much about the functions of the family in the education and spiritual formation of children that we could profitably review. This is a matter we obviously need to think and pray about.

Tension Regarding Standards—The question of standards appropriate to the Adventist lifestyle looms immensely higher on the horizon of young people than it does for us older folks. Forty percent of young Adventists in the Valuegenesis study felt that "the emphasis on Adventist rules and standards is so strong that the message of Christianity gets lost."[12]

The survey reveals that many feel there is imbalance and failure to differentiate between major and minor matters. This is especially so with regard to adornment, recreational activities, and the movies.[13] And further, it is generally felt that standards are more strictly enforced in church and school than they are at home. Particularly is this the case regarding clothes, jewelry, music, and entertainment. The young people perceive a double standard here that practically amounts to hypocrisy.[14]

The Valuegenesis study concludes: "It is evident that . . . extensive negative feelings exist concerning how Adventists use, emphasize, and enforce standards, and this alienation is closely related to a number of undesirable attitudes and behaviors that may signal the eventual abandonment of the church and the faith."[15] Many of our young adults "do not possess, in the words of Ellen White, 'a settling into the truth, both intellectually and spiritually, so they cannot be moved' [manuscript 173, 1902]."[16]

They warn: "Make no mistake. How we handle church standards is the crucial issue in the determination of whether or not we will retain the rising generation in the church. Acceptance of Adventist standards was the second most important variable in the entire study in predicting whether or not the students intended to remain as Adventists by age 40 and the most important in determining denominational loyalty. Rules and standards are the 'stickiest' point in the whole youth value arena, or, as I like to suggest, it is 'the hinge of retention.'"[17]

Again, this is a challenging and complex matter. On the one hand, the tension between home and institution may be partly a result of the drift on the part of Adventist families in the direction of the wider society. On the other hand, maybe the church has failed to reassess and validate adequately the standards it advocates. And there is tension within the church between those who advocate stronger enforcement and those who favor reassessment, and between those who feel the family should take more responsibility and those who feel the school should be the major vehicle of enforcement. The "blaming" I hear is utterly unproductive. We are the church, and it would seem that these studies should jolt us awake and drive us to prayer, study, and action.

Young Adventists and the Church—The Valuegenesis study probed the church experience of young Adventists.[18] Only 44 percent felt that the local congregation was warm and accepting, and the older the students, the less warmth they perceived. Only about a third felt that the church challenged their thinking and taught them a lot, and merely 28 percent felt that they were encouraged to ask questions. To make matters worse, Adventist young people were less positive about the church in these respects than were those who attended Southern Baptist and other mainline churches.

If the experience of young Adventists in our congregations is not more warm and stimulating than these responses indicate, how long will they attend? Why do they experience so little of the joy and vibrancy of the gospel in our churches? Why in a secular age such as ours, when the great questions of meaning and purpose in life loom so large, is there felt to be so little that is stimulating about the answers the church gives?

Herein lies an immense challenge to every member. Surely all of us must do all we can to generate a more caring and vibrant climate in the church. If there is validity to the Valuegenesis study, then perhaps we should not be shocked by what the editor of the *Adventist Review* writes: "The Adventist Church in North America is suffering staggering losses among its young people. How large the numbers are, nobody seems to know, nor are most leaders eager to know because the statistics would be discouraging. For many of our youth, their graduation from academy or college marks their 'graduation' from church life also—they effectively drop out."[19]

But shock is not enough. It is time for us to think and pray and do.

National Concern

The general failure of American society to transmit to its young people an adequate sense of meaning to life in a moral universe is now recognized as a major national concern. Many societies and organizations have arisen that seek to address the problem at its most basic level—that of the family: the Family Research Council, Concerned Women for America, Promise Keepers, James Dobson's Focus on the Family, the establishment of centers for marriage and family studies at evangelical colleges, and a large variety and number of family enrichment programs.

The Adventist Church, too, has recently taken serious measures to foster the spiritual and moral growth of young people and involve them in many of the interesting and challenging activities of the church.

What can individual members do to contribute toward a solution? A few suggestions for study and discussion follow.

• Foster study sessions that create awareness of the gravity of the situation.

• Rethink and advocate ways of making family devotional/learning sessions inspiring and meaningful for all.

• Generate interest in, and support for, family enrichment-style seminars in larger churches or groups of churches.

• Participate in study groups to find ways of making the activities and worship services of the church more interesting and challenging to young people.

• Make young people feel welcome in the congregation and give them responsibilities.

---

[1] The data and descriptions of the family given here and in succeeding sections of this chapter relate to the family in the United States. Circumstances may be quite different in other places and societies. It is not possible to generalize for the entire world. Readers are invited to compare the situation in

their country with that in the United States.

[2] Charles C. Crider and Robert C. Kistler, *The Seventh-day Adventist Family: An Empirical Study* (Berrien Springs, Mich.: Andrews University Press, 1979), p. 247.

[3] *Ibid.,* pp. 77, 78.

[4] *Ibid.,* p. 78.

[5] Roger L. Dudley with V. Bailey Gillespie, *Valuegenesis: Faith in the Balance* (Riverside, Calif.: La Sierra University Press, 1992).

[6] *Ibid.,* p. 20.

[7] *Ibid.,* p. 21.

[8] *Ibid.,* p. 25.

[9] Crider and Kistler, p. 66.

[10] Dudley, pp. 44, 198-201.

[11] Crider and Kistler, pp. 67, 68.

[12] Dudley, p. 51.

[13] *Ibid.,* p. 150.

[14] *Ibid.,* pp. 156-159.

[15] *Ibid.,* p. 155.

[16] *Ibid.,* p. 160.

[17] *Ibid.,* p. 147.

[18] *Ibid.,* pp. 169-173.

[19] William G. Johnsson, *The Fragmenting of Adventism* (Boise, Idaho: Pacific Press Pub. Assn., 1995), p. 52.

CHAPTER 11

How Are We Today?

The title of this chapter asks us to look inward and take stock of the spiritual state of our lives and of the church as we come to the turning point of the centuries. But this is not a simple thing to do, for the question arises as to how one is to gain sufficient objectivity and an appropriate sense of perspective in order to do so in any sense that has validity. The world is much with us and crowds in upon our consciousness and so forms the framework of our thought and judgment that, apart from the guidance of the Holy Spirit, it is well-nigh impossible for us to see ourselves in the light of eternity.

The perennial human challenge of seeing our lives and actions from the vantage point of the gospel and allowing it to judge our thoughts and actions is ever before us. Special occasions such as this when we prepare to ring out the old century and enter the new spur us to do so more conscientiously than we are wont to do in the usual course of our lives.

Many passages of Scripture address this challenge in one way or another. They remind us of our shortsightedness, vulnerability to deceptions of various kinds, and proneness to be less than fully awake to the significance of events about us and of our own state vis-à-vis eternity.

In a sense this takes us back to the overall theme of the Seventh-day Adventist Church and today's world. All the chapters in this book, in one way or another, have to do with both church and world. In most we have thought of the world as the world of mission—as the people who have yet to hear the message. We enlarged upon this challenge in chapter 2, in which we examined some of the major opportunities and obstacles facing the church in its task of proclaiming the three angels' messages to all peoples of earth. And in chapter 9 we thought of the fulfillment of this challenge in two ways—by going out to those who have not yet heard the good news and by cultivating such a foretaste of the coming kingdom within the fellowship of the community of faith that others are drawn into our midst.

In this chapter, however, we will be thinking of ourselves and the world and the church in a different sense. Our thought revolves here around what might be called the duality of our lives. As Christians we live and have our being in this world, and much of what we are—our patterns of life and thought—is strongly influenced by this wider world. But we are primarily citizens of the City of God, and that citizenship defines the meaning and purpose of our lives and the values by which we live.

Our concern with the world in this chapter revolves around the challenge we face of maintaining our Christian perspective in a secular society that intrudes upon our thought and makes enormous demands upon our time and energies. All of which threatens to nudge our higher citizenship from the determining center it should occupy in our lives.

Much of what you have just read sounds rather individualistic. And, of course, our discipleship always involves individual as well as corporate responses, but in this chapter we seek to encourage thought about our corporate response, as a community of faith, to the pressures of the contemporary world. The question before us is How can we maintain the status of a community that consciously and truly reflects the values of the gospel in thought and deed even as we seek to sustain healthy and positive relationships in our citizenship in the wider world?

The Adventist Church has been described by several sociologists as a primary society. By this they mean that, for Adventists, religious belief and authority is determinative for all issues of life. Religion is not limited to a designated sector of experience; it is not merely one of an assortment of factors on the basis of which important life-decisions are made. Instead it is the determining factor. Commitment to God and the fulfillment of His purposes is the absolute that relativizes all earthly concerns and relationships. The Adventist Church has traditionally been a community that fosters the maintenance and transmission of this hierarchy of allegiance and value. Hence its designation as a primary society.

The question is whether this pattern can be maintained in the face of a pervasive, widely different, and competing set of values. And if so, how this can be achieved? The purpose of this discussion is to help us gain perspective as we think about and discuss such matters. We need to ask ourselves whether our corporate experience and witness fulfills the internal and external roles it should.

The Scriptural Basis for Discussion

Two of Jesus' Warnings—Jesus' warnings against false prophets in the concluding section of the Sermon on the Mount (Matt. 7:15-20) is one of a series of general warnings that have permanent validity for the church. False teachers and teachings of all kinds there have always been and always will be, and there are many warnings against such in the Scriptures. Some of these distortions of the faith are obvious. Others, like the Gnosticism against which the early church contested, are extremely subtle. Some relate to a specific teaching or doctrine; others reflect the spirit of an age.

Jesus employed an agrarian parable in providing guidance against deceptions. "You will know them by their fruits" (verse 16). The standard by which the fruits are to be judged is surely the kind of goodness expounded in the preceding sections of the Sermon on the Mount. In a sense the sermon adumbrates the essence of this entire chapter—it upholds a standard that enables us to see ourselves in the light of true goodness.

The warnings of Matthew 24 relate more specifically to the

latter days of earth's history. The disciples asked Jesus: "Tell us, when will this be, and what will be the sign of your coming and of the end of the age" (verse 3).

Jesus warned the disciples: "Beware that no one leads you astray" (verse 4), for there will be false messiahs and false prophets who will mislead many. The disciples expected the great Messianic event of the ages to take place almost immediately. In response, Jesus extended the timetable—"the end is not yet" (verse 6).

It would seem that our concerns regarding the Second Coming are precisely the opposite of those original followers of the Master. Generally, the eschatological issues we wrestle with do not relate to time-setting or an overzealous expectation of an immediate end to this present age. Our besetment is a lack of concern and the loss of a sense of urgency. We get so caught up in the things of this world that the vision of the land of glory grows dim.

The point I wish to make here is that again, as in the Sermon on the Mount, Jesus issued a warning to His followers—both generally and in regard to specific issues His followers are to be alert to lest they be misled. The concern that prompted the disciples to inquire about the time of the coming of the kingdom is precisely the opposite of the spirit of our age. But the "beware" of the Master is just as applicable to us (perhaps it should ring even more loudly in our ears), even though it points to a very different danger.

A Warning From the Apostle Paul—Paul issued a call to the Roman Christians to "wake from sleep" (Rom. 13:11), for the day of light is near. This message is located in an eschatological setting in which this present world is symbolized by "night" and "darkness"and the world that is to come, by "day" and "light" (verse 12). The state of mind of the Christians in Rome, as is revealed in this passage, is the opposite of that of the Palestinian Christians of Matthew 24. Unlike them, the Romans needed to be jarred awake to the reality of the coming kingdom. Paul's admonition to them is entirely appropriate to us, for we are much more like these Romans than we are like the Palestinians. The Romans were advised to govern their lives by the light that shines from the kingdom which is to come (Rom. 13:14) and to rise above the kinds of things characteristic of the world of night and darkness.

The question as to how Christians in any age and time and under any circumstances can gain perspective to judge adequately the ethos—morals, beliefs, and attitudes—of their society is partially answered here. Paul's word to the Romans is that they should see their world, the world of night and darkness, in the light of that world of day and light that is to come.

If we apply this to our own experience, it calls us to immerse ourselves in the Scriptures and the gospel until the beauty of the day of light is so clear before our eyes that we can see and judge the values and ways of this dark world in the light of this heavenly vision.

The "Mount of Vision"—The message to the angel of the church in Laodicea merits more detailed attention than we have given the above passages, if for no other reason than that from their inception Adventists have been convinced that the letters refer to the churches in historical sequence and that the message to the Laodiceans has a special application to them.

It seems to me there was much more frequent reference to this letter, in appeals and admonitions to the church, in my youth than at present. This is perhaps because it is such a sobering message and most of us prefer to hear "smooth" words. But there are two sides to the letter. Although it does contain one of the severest judgments in the series of letters, it is also one of the most encouraging and personal. It culminates in the warmth of a fellowship meal with Christ and the promise of a place at God's throne. This would seem to be an appropriate time for us to take a fresh look as some aspects of this message.

The letters were written, in the first instance, to Christians in the Roman province of Asia Minor—to some of the same people addressed in Peter's letter. The imperial cult had been elevated to a high level in Asia. This made the practice of Christianity difficult, and Christians were undergoing stress and hardship. The future of Christianity in the land did not look bright. The letters counter this dismaying outlook and present a powerful picture of God as the Lord of history, of Christ as the Redeemer of humankind, and of the ultimate fulfillment of God's purposes in the soon-coming kingdom.

Each of the letters concludes with the redeemed living in fellowship with Christ in that other world, and the letter to Thyatira concludes with the promise that everyone who overcomes will be given "authority over the nations; to rule them with an iron rod" (Rev. 2:26, 27). These must have seemed to be strange promises to those suffering legal disabilities and persecution because of their religious profession.

These letters have been interpreted as having a dual application. "Although the various messages to the seven churches must have applied in the first instance to the churches of Asia in John's own time, they were also relevant to the future history of the church. . . . A study of history reveals that these messages are, indeed, applicable in a special way to seven periods that cover the entire history of the church."[1]

If this letter is addressed to us, the question then arises as to its meaning in our time and place in history. There are wide differences between the circumstances and social location of the Laodicean Christians and our own, and yet there are important parallels.

Despite the straitened circumstances of their lives, some of the Laodiceans were apparently becoming materially prosperous. "You say, 'I am rich, I have prospered, and I need nothing'" (Rev. 3:17).

It is tempting to speculate about the reasons for this surprising development, especially since it has been a recurring phenomenon in the history of Christianity. The Adventist upward mobility syndrome constitutes a notable example of this. The cause is exceedingly complex and cannot be analyzed here. Suffice it to say that Christianity induces consciousness of a moral universe, and those who look forward to the coming kingdom order their lives with a purpose that makes them faithful stewards of earthly as well as of heavenly things.

Of course, the prosperous may easily become so engrossed with the things of this earth that the vision of the heavenly city grows dim. This seems to have become the case with some of the Laodiceans. Exactly how they managed to become prosperous under such difficult circumstances is a conundrum. However, marginalized people have been known to rise to surprising heights. Wesley lamented that this was the case with many Methodists. As a result of their diligence and uprightness, many became prosperous, and with prosperity came a reduced concern regarding things heavenly. From a sociological point of view it would be surprising if both of the above phenomena were not evident among Adventists.

The Laodiceans were told rather sharply that they did not realize that they were "wretched, pitiable, poor, blind, and naked" (verse 17). They were materially self-sufficient but had become spiritually impoverished. And more significant, they were blind to the reality of their spiritual state of being. This is a perennial challenge to most Christians, including ourselves.

One of Ellen White's comments about the Laodicean letter is titled "The Mount of Vision." She states: "If every man who has influence could ascend some mount of vision from which he could behold all his works as Christ beholds them when He declares, 'I know thy works'; if the laborer could trace from cause to effect every objectionable word and act, the sight would be more than he could bear."[2]

The function of a letter like this to the Laodiceans is that it stops us in our tracks, as it were, and lifts us up to a "mount of vision" from which we can take stock of our lives and see ourselves in the light of the kingdom. From this mount we are enabled to see again that our God is the Lord of history, who is preparing to bring the purposes of His creation to fulfillment in a new kingdom.

Jesus stands at the door and knocks. His first great promise to those who grant Him entrance is: "I will come in and sit down to supper with him and he with me" (verse 20, NEB). This beautiful promise points to a fellowship meal. It conveys a beautiful sense of intimacy—those with whom Christ dines are not strangers to Him. But it is more than a fellowship meal. He will feed us with the bread of heaven until our souls are fully nourished.

The second great promise lifts us to the mount of vision. It drives thought back to the cosmic victory of Christ over the powers of darkness, lifts it up to the enthronement of the resurrected Christ at the right hand of God on the heavenly throne, and points it forward to that day when "to the one who conquers I will give a place with me on my throne" (verse 21).

From the mount of vision provided by this letter, we are encouraged to see and measure our lives on earth in perspective. We see human history in the light of divine history, events on earth in the light of the kingdom to come, human time in the light of eternity, and our lives on earth in the light of God's purposes for His redeemed children. The vision thus gained serves to relativize what seems to be utterly important in the here and now and enables us to direct our lives and order our priorities better in terms of the ultimate goal.

Some Secular Witnesses

Contemporary thought leaders in various disciplines, most noticeably in sociology and education, have published analysis that in a different kind of way hold up a mirror which helps us to see ourselves in clearer perspective than we sometimes do.

For instance, Allan Bloom, professor of history at the University of Chicago, sounds almost like a prophet of Israel in his analysis of some of the causes of the social malaise of contemporary society. He indicts several social institutions, including the church, university, and especially the family, for failing to inculcate the moral values and sense of purpose that lie at the foundation of a stable society.

"The other element of fundamental primary learning that has disappeared is religion. . . . It was the home—and the houses of worship related to it—where religion lived. The holy days and the common language and set of references that permeated most households constituted a large part of the family bond and gave it substantial content. Moses and the Tables of the Law, Jesus and His preaching of brotherly love, had an imaginative existence. Passages from the Psalms and the Gospels echoed in children's heads. Attending church or synagogue, praying at the table, were a way of life, inseparable from the moral education that was supposed to be the family's special responsibility in this democracy. Actually, the moral teaching was the religious teaching. . . . The things one was supposed to do, the sense that the world supported them and punished disobedience, were all incarnated in the biblical stories. The loss of the gripping inner life vouchsafed those who were nurtured by the Bible must be primarily attributed not to the schools or political life, but to the family, which, with all its rights to privacy, has proved unable to maintain any content of its own. The dreariness of the family's spiritual landscape passes belief. . . . The delicate fabric of the civilization into which the successive generations are woven has unraveled, and children are raised, not educated."[3]

In *Habits of the Heart,* which is one of the most thoroughgoing analyses of the American national character to date, Robert Bellah, professor of sociology at the University of California at Berkeley, and his coauthors are hardly less strident regarding the failure of contemporary society to inculcate a sense of meaning and purpose and morality. Their observations regarding the lack of seriousness with which the mandates of the divine are taken parallel the biblical description of the Laodiceans. Yes, people still attend church in America, but the religion they profess lacks determinative influence.

"Today religion represents a frame of reference for the self as conspicuous in its absence as in its presence. To be sure, more than nine out of ten Americans 'believe in God,' surveys report, and four out of ten attend church regularly. . . . But relatively few middle-class urbanites described themselves to us as 'children of God,' created in His image and likeness, bound by His commandments, and inspired by His love.

"Following on the heels of liberalized religion's relaxed sense of duty, authority, and virtue comes the rejection of institutional religion itself."[4]

They describe the "cultural standards" that obtain and the kind of person that results. "For those oriented primarily to upward mobility, to 'success,' major features of American society appear to be the 'normal outcome of the operation of individual achievement.' In this conception, individuals, unfettered by family or other group affiliation, are given the chance to make the best of themselves, and, though equality of opportunity is essential, inequality of result is 'natural.' . . . The only clearly defined cultural standards against which status can be measured are the gross standards of income, consumption, and conformity to rational procedures for attaining ends."[5]

And finally, they describe the result of contemporary "cultural standards" regarding status and individualism, etc., as leading the nation to the "very brink of disaster." "For several centuries we have embarked on a great effort to increase our freedom, wealth and power. For over a hundred years, a large part of the American people, the middle class, has imagined that the virtual meaning of life lies in the acquisition of ever-increasing status, income, and authority, from which genuine freedom is supposed to come. Our achievements have been enormous. . . . Yet we seem to be hovering on the very brink of disaster, not only from international conflict, but from the internal incoherence of our own society."[6]

It is not surprising that these and other studies have aroused the national consciousness. Lack of space prevents comment and analysis of these studies. They are quoted to provoke reflection on our orientation to life and society and to help provide a pathway up the mount of vision.

Christian Assurance

We have been invited to examine our personal and corporate discipleship from the mount of vision, which shall enable us to see things in the light of the kingdom of heaven. Because the things and patterns of thought of the wider world push in upon us, it is good for us to keep reminding ourselves that our God is the Lord of history and to undergo the salutary experience of examining ourselves in the light of heaven. This experience should call us back to a closer walk with our Lord—and we walk with assurance. Neither untoward event nor personal failure deflect us from the way, for He is our Saviour, and His power will sustain us to the end.

We close with a passage from the letter to the Hebrews: "My righteous one will live by faith. . . . We are not among those who shrink back and so are lost, but among those who have faith and so are saved" (Heb. 10:38, 39).

---

[1] *The Seventh-day Adventist Bible Commentary* (Washington, D.C.: Review and Herald Pub. Assn., 1953-1957), vol. 7, p. 737.

[2] *Ibid.,* Ellen G. White Comments, vol. 7, p. 963.

[3] Allan Bloom, *The Closing of the American Mind* (New York: Simon and Schuster, 1987), pp. 56, 57.

[4] Robert N. Bellah et al., eds., *Habits of the Heart: Individualism and Commitment in American Life* (Berkeley, Calif.: University of California, 1985), pp. 63, 64.

[5] *Ibid.,* pp. 148, 149.

[6] *Ibid.,* p. 284.

CHAPTER 12

Strong and Active for the Final Crisis

In chapter 11 we were invited to engage in introspective thought regarding our standing as Christians in a materialistic and secular world. We sought to take stock of our discipleship and of the basic orientation of our lives. It was suggested that some of Jesus' warnings, the Sermon on the Mount, and the letter to the Laodiceans constitute a "mount of vision" from which we can see our lives on this earth in the light of the kingdom of heaven. We went further and suggested that analyses of American society by some social scientists hold up a mirror that helps us take an honest look at ourselves.

By and large this search for clarity of thought and vision to penetrate the plethora of concerns that crowd in upon us like a haze has been an intellectual undertaking. Certainly correct belief is foundational to the Christian life. And clarity of thought in explicating God's revelation as faithfully as is humanly possible is essential to an intelligent profession of the Christian faith. But there is more to Christian discipleship than intellectual conviction, and assent to doctrine alone does not necessarily make one a disciple of the Master.

In this chapter we change to a different axis of thought to explore some dimensions and functions of the experiential aspect of discipleship. There must obviously be conscious intellectual commitment, but Christian experience, although somewhat nebulous and difficult to define, is also utterly important in the Christian life. The Christian who would be strong and active today, every day, and in the time of crisis needs both a clear view of the purposes of our Lord in history and an abiding sense of living in His presence. The key passages we will be examining come from Paul's letter to the Christians at Ephesus and from the Second Letter of Peter.

Ephesians, perhaps more than any other, is the book of the church in the New Testament. It portrays Christians as being "built together spiritually into a dwelling place for God" (Eph. 2:22) and suggests that they can understand the depths of the love of Christ and come "to know it, though it is beyond knowledge" (Eph. 3:19, NEB). In reading Ephesians one comes to feel that there is here an experience that transcends the boundaries of knowledge.

The Second Letter of Peter, like the first, strongly emphasizes the eschatological hope of the gospel. In the ladder of virtue that we will consider and in other passages, it strongly upholds a standard of Christian moral life over against the laxness of a permissive pagan society. The whole letter is grounded in the ambiance of the kind of experience that transformed the great fisherman from the disciple of the betrayal to the resolute apostle of the early church.

The Importance of Religious Experience

Several years ago I listened to a lecture by a noted anthropologist on the topic of church renewal. He said, "There are always three basic dimensions in the religious experience of humankind. First, there are those things that are believed; second, all religions define the moral life in one way or another; and third, there is the element of experience." Then, in a paraphrase of 1 Corinthians 13, he said, "And the greatest of these three is experience." He went on to suggest that it was precisely here that the Christian church is the weakest. He observed that much time has been spent in teaching Christian doctrine and in admonishing people regarding an appropriate Christian lifestyle, but that not nearly enough effort has been made to bring persons into the presence of the living God.

This message was brought home to me about the same time in a meeting with several anthropologists. Upon discovering that I was an Adventist, one said, "I know Adventists in several of the islands. You produce a schoolroom religion." Another responded, "This is remarkable. I have seen the same thing in Africa." The inference of this is that we do well in inculcating orderliness and teaching doctrine, but that our corporate worship services are almost devoid of the more expressive manifestations of the religious life.

The point I wish to make here relates to the weight given by many social scientists to the element of experience in the practice of religion. If even limited credence is given to this observation, the question that arises relates to the level and adequacy of experience in the Adventist Church. And what about the rather specific observation that the emphasis in Adventism is rather heavy upon correct belief and appropriate behavior and lifestyle with proportionately less attention to experience?

And finally, if it is felt that more positive attention to experience would help make us stronger and more active Christians, then how can this be achieved and what elements of experience would be helpful to us? Some suggestions will be made in an attempt to answer these questions later in this chapter.

Living in the Presence of God

Thinking of the experiential dimensions of religion almost inevitably takes my thought to Luther's Large Catechism.[1] It consists of a presentation of the faith in five sections as taught in: God's commandments, the Apostles' creed, the Lord's Prayer, baptism, and the Lord's Supper.

In the first paragraph of the catechism Luther states the first commandment: "Thou shalt have no other gods before me" (Ex. 20:3). And then he immediately turns it into a question. "What do these words mean? . . . What is it to have a god?" He answers: "As I have often said, the confidence and faith of the heart alone make both God and an idol. . . . Whatever your heart clings to and confides in, that is really your God."[2]

What kind of creed is this? There is no attempt to tell who God is; no metaphysical statement describing the divine perfections or attributes of God; nothing about the Trinity; nothing about the work of God as Creator, Preserver, and Saviour of humankind; nothing even about graven images, which was a lively issue in the Lutheran Reformation. There is not a hint of the intellectual question regarding evidences of the existence of God. Luther will have none of these. His concern here is more fundamental, more simple, and yet immensely more profound. The issue for Luther is not theological; it is the religious or experiential response that he is concerned about.

Luther is far from questioning the existence or reality of God. Quite the opposite. This is assumed in every line he writes. What he is teaching is that knowledge is not enough. As he says, the devil knows that there is a God and trembles—but he *has* no god. It may be so with us. He says: "To have a god is simply to trust and believe in one with our whole heart."[3] He gives examples of the idols we trust in: riches, which "is a universal idol on earth," and "great skill, wisdom, power, and influence, friends and honors."[4]

He closes the section on the first commandment with an admonition: "Examine your own heart diligently and inquire of it, and you will surely find whether or no it cleaves to God alone."[5]

The theme of personal response to, and living in the presence of, God continues throughout the catechism. For instance, after quoting the first line of the Apostles' Creed, "I believe in God the Father Almighty, Creator of heaven and earth,"[6] he asks what these words mean and then answers: "I believe that I am God's creature."[7] And this, of course, is the basis of a relationship—God is truly our Creator-Father, and we are truly His children.

Then there follows the section on the Lord's Prayer, which he says "begins in heaven, comes down to earth, our daily bread, and then returns with us to heaven."[8] He describes the naturalness and personal experience of prayer for a Christian.

The section on baptism and the Lord's Supper are of a piece

with the whole. There is an emphasis in both on nearness to God. Of course, Luther is concerned with correct belief, but what impresses one throughout the whole is the emphasis on a personal relationship, commitment, and experience.

A Dwelling Place for God (Eph. 2:19-22)—The grandeur of the vision of God's purpose and the beauty of oneness *in Christ* portrayed in Ephesians are awe-inspiring. The letter is from "Paul, [who writes from prison in Rome] an apostle of Christ Jesus *by the will of God.*" He uses three terms to describe the recipients of the letter. They are the *saints,* who are also *faithful,* and they are *"in Christ Jesus"* (Eph. 1:1). This final phrase of the first verse is perhaps the key expression of the Epistle (see chapter 4) and sets the tone for the whole. To be "in Christ" is to be personally united to Christ, the head of the body, and therefore also to the other members of the body. Much of the Epistle is a development of these two relationships—vertically with Christ and horizontally within the community of faith.

Three images are employed in this passage to describe God's new society:

A. *Citizens of God's Kingdom (Eph. 2:19).* They are described as having been stateless, aliens, not members of the commonwealth of Israel (verse 12), but now are citizens. The contrast here is between the dereliction of statelessness and the sense of identity and purpose that comes from belonging to God's kingdom.

B. *Members of the Household of God (Eph. 2:19).* Their sense of identity and relationship is here enormously magnified. To be citizens of a state is one thing, but to be members of a noted family, as they are in Christ, is quite another. And again the relationship points in two directions—to God the Father, with whom the children have a privileged relationship, and to the ties binding brothers and sisters in the faith together.

C. *A Holy Temple—A Dwelling Place for God (Eph. 2:20-22).* Here a more specifically religious/spiritual emphasis is given. First, the building has a foundation. The Old Testament (the prophets) and the New Testament (the apostles) constitute the foundation documents of the church. Jesus Christ is the cornerstone, in whom "the whole structure is joined together and grows" (verse 21). Unity and growth (referring to growth in grace rather than numbers) are here closely connected, and Christ is the key to both.

Finally, the capstone is added to the composite portrait. The church (community) is the dwelling place of God in the Spirit (verse 22).

This portrait constitutes an enormous challenge to the contemporary church. How well do we fulfill the vision of a single new humanity that transcends all human barriers? How conscious are we of our heavenly citizenship, and to what extent does it constitute the determinative orientation in our lives? Do we conceive of the church as the dwelling place of God in the Spirit? And to what extent are we consciously aware of the presence of God in our worship?

Called to Do Battle (Eph. 6:10-18)—We must pass by, albeit with reluctance, the most beautiful prayer in the Bible (Eph. 3:14-20), apart from the Lord's Prayer, and Paul's subsequent admonitions regarding unity. Leaving the magnificent beauty of these themes, Paul brings us face-to-face with the harsh realities of evil in this world (Eph. 6:10-18). The change is abrupt and reminds us that the period between the comings of our Lord is one of conflict. It is as if Paul now issues a strident call to battle.

A. *The Enemy We Face (Eph. 6:10-12)*—The three major characteristics of the principalities and powers that oppose us are: They are powerful, wicked, and cunning. How, then, can we prevail against them? The apostle gives two general admonitions. The first is "Be strong in the Lord and in the strength of his power" (verse 10). The second is to "put on the whole armor of God" (verse 11). Here we see the maintenance of a balance between reliance upon divine enablement and power, and an appeal to human resources of strength and wisdom.

B. *The Armor of God (Eph. 6:13-18)*—Paul here builds an analogy based upon the six main pieces of a soldier's equipment:

the belt (truth), the breastplate (righteousness), boots (good news of peace), the shield (faith), helmet (salvation), and the sword (the Word of God). We are to "pray . . . at all times" (verse 18)—not merely sometimes. Finally, we are to "keep alert" (verse 18). This reflects the warning of Jesus Himself to the disciples to be watchful regarding the unexpectedness of His return and the onset of temptation.

The passage closes on a magnificent personal note. Paul is in chains, facing trial in Rome. He requests the Church of Ephesus to pray for him, not that he might be released, but that he may boldly and clearly make known God's hidden purpose (in the imperial palace) (verses 19, 20).

Peter (2 Peter 1:5-11)—In a sense, 2 Peter 1:5-11 is parallel to Paul's great summons to vigilance. The Second Coming had been expected during the lifetime of the first Christians. That generation was now passing, and the opponents of Christianity argued that this constituted evidence that the hope of the Parousia was mistaken. Their eschatological skepticism was grounded in rational arguments regarding the improbability of divine intervention in human history. In addition, they seem to have endorsed a moral libertinism and denied the concept of divine judgment.

Peter warns against all of this and provides counterarguments. Primary emphasis in the letter is on Jesus, beginning with the affirmation that "His divine power has given us everything needed for life and godliness" (2 Peter 1:3). Therefore, we may escape the corruption that is in the world and "become participants of the divine nature" (verse 4).

Next, and again in a sense parallel to Paul's panoply of armor, Peter lists a series of virtues that Christians should consciously build into their lives: faith, goodness, knowledge, self-control, endurance, godliness, mutual affection, love (see verses 5-7). These keep the Christian from being "ineffective and unfruitful" (verse 8). There is a danger that Christians may be "nearsighted and blind" (verse 9). Finally, assurance is given that "entry into the eternal kingdom of our Lord and Savior Jesus

Christ will be richly provided for you" (verse 11).

The above tantalizingly brief survey of these passages serves to remind us of the cosmic dimensions of evil and of our constant need for vigilance and renewal. Both Paul and Peter repeatedly call their readers to a renewed vision and experience of God. As Paul wrote to the Corinthians: "We have this treasure in earthen vessels" (2 Cor. 4:7). The full intent of this analogy is that such vessels are porous—they leak. The contents run out and get cold. They need to be constantly refilled. So it is with us. An erstwhile enthusiastic commitment may become nominal unless it is nurtured and fed. We need the ministry of the Holy Spirit working within our hearts and within the Christian community to lift us into God's presence. This brings us back to a consideration of the place of experience in religion introduced at the beginning of this chapter. We now make a dramatic shift and consider experience from an academic point of view.

The Power of Religious Experience

The following diagram is used by some students of religion to show the proportional weight of intellect and experience in religion.[9]

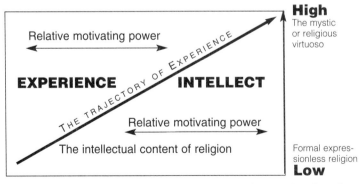

Diagram of the trajectory of religious experience showing the proportional motivating power of intellect and experience.

The base line represents the intellectual content of the religious experience. This is a defining guiding force. The importance of the belief system can hardly be exaggerated, for there can be no lasting commitment—especially in our rational, secular world—without a firm conviction that the truth of the things believed can be rationally demonstrated.

The vertical line represents the element of experience. At the low end is what might be called a rational form of religion dominated by cold intellect. The experience of a mystic—one caught up into the presence of God in a beatific vision—would be near the top.

The human response to experience in religion is deep and sensitive. On the one hand, those accustomed to a relatively high level of experiential involvement will not be religiously satisfied by more formal forms of expression lower down the scale. On the other hand, those accustomed to low experience/rational styles of worship may be uneasy about what seems to them to be undue enthusiasm. We have seen examples of both in the Adventist Church. We have failed to retain and satisfy groups from exuberant African independent churches because of the low level of experience in our services, and on the other hand, in this country some have found the worship of celebration churches distasteful.

Students of religion are interested in the relationship between the intellect and experience represented by the oblique line within the box. The experience of the great thirteenth-century theologian Thomas Aquinas provides an example of this. After writing great theological tomes, for which he was awarded the title "Doctor of the Church," he received a mystical vision and stopped writing. Some of his biographers account for this dramatic change by pointing to the magnificence of the beatific vision he had received. So sublime were the things of God he had experienced and in comparison so poor and beggarly the things he had written that he could not bring himself to write any more. This is a striking illustration of one aspect of the power of experience.

In the view of these scholars, belief tests and defines the parameters of experience, but the driving force that gives power to conviction is experience. All of this needs to be placed in context. Most scholars of religion know, even better than most Christian religious leaders, that religion is the most powerful motivating/legitimating force in the world. And they believe that in one way or another experience is the force that fires the religious spirit and keeps it burning brightly.

Strong and Active—The Role of Experience—The passages of Scripture referred to in this chapter lead to the conviction that established belief and a strong sense of living in the presence of God are both essential elements in the Christian life. Adventist doctrine is grounded in Scripture and has been clearly defined. And the presentation of the message in our evangelistic and mission work has been intellectually compelling. In general we have specialized in the intellectual dimensions of what it means to be an Adventist. It is not as clear, however, that we have fostered the experiential dimensions of the faith in an equally satisfying manner.

To be strong and active requires both burning hearts and enlightened minds. If we can join a deepened experience of the presence of the divine in our lives to our already strong convictions, we should be both stronger and more active in our discipleship. Let us then briefly consider the role of experience—subservient, of course, to correct knowledge—and some of the ways in which this can be meaningful to us.

Perhaps we should think first of all of our worship services. Can we generate a stronger sense of coming into the presence of God and worshiping with the full depths of our being? Perhaps services should be geared less toward the imparting of knowledge and more toward praise and congregational participation in acts of worship. Can we cultivate a deeper awareness of God's holiness and greatness and our finitude and need as we worship?

Second, there is a danger that we are forgetting how to celebrate the Sabbath. Or perhaps we have become so preoccupied with the significance of the Sabbath in the great controversy that we are losing sight of its experiential religious significance. How wonderful it is to close out the work of the week and seek the blessings of the Lord in holy time! Consciousness of entering holy time deepens our experience of worshiping a holy God on the holy Sabbath day. Surely we could cultivate a deeper sense of entering the presence of God with acts of praise on this day.

Third, I think we could gain a much greater blessing from our celebration of the Lord's Supper than we do. We're almost proud of our conviction that the bread and wine are symbols and do not become the body and blood of our Lord. That is true, but we all but lose sight of the presence of Christ at the table.

Ellen White writes: "It is at these, His own appointments, that Christ meets His people, and energizes them by His presence. . . . Christ is there to minister to His children. All who come with their faith fixed upon Him will be greatly blessed." [10]

"The ordinances that point to our Lord's humiliation and suffering are regarded too much as a form. . . . Our senses need to be quickened to lay hold of the mystery of godliness. . . . The service forms a living connection by which the believer is bound up with Christ, and thus bound up with the Father. In a special sense it forms a connection between dependent human beings and God." [11]

Those who take these words seriously receive a great blessing at the table of our Lord.

Fourth, we do very little to celebrate the great events in the life of our Lord Jesus. There is a reason, of course. Many feel that both the rituals and dates are tainted by paganism. And so we do nothing. We do not celebrate the Incarnation—that miracle of all miracles—or the glorious resurrection of our Lord, or His ascension into heaven. Would not some celebration rekindle a sense of awe at these great wonders? Is there not something we can do to make these a part of our experience?

And finally, there are many other things we can do to renew and deepen our experience. Bible study and prayer support groups continue to be a blessing to many. Camp meetings and regional meetings provide special opportunities for fellowship as well as spiritual renewal. Participating in soul winning provides opportunity for unique kinds of experiences. Bible reading and prayer in private devotions can be greatly enriching. Many passages that I read and reread have been deeply rewarding to me.

As we approach the last Sabbath of the millennium, let us bow our heads in prayer for a deeper experience of the things of our Lord.

_____

[1] *Dr. Martin Luther's Large Catechism* (Minneapolis: Augsburg Publishing House, 1935), p. 44.

[2] *Ibid.*, p. 44.

[3] *Ibid.*

[4] *Ibid.*, p. 45.

[5] *Ibid.*, p. 48.

[6] *Ibid.*, p. 113.

[7] *Ibid.*, p. 114.

[8] *Ibid.*, p. 138.

[9] I am indebted to Huston Smith for this diagram. He drew it in a lecture I heard several years ago. I have heard it referred to by others, but have not seen it in print.

[10] Ellen G. White, *The Desire of Ages* (Mountain View, Calif.: Pacific Press Pub. Assn., 1898), p. 656.

[11] *Ibid.*, pp. 660, 661.

CHAPTER 13

The Heavenly Family

Like me you have probably grown tired of all the hype associated with the ending of the twentieth century. Yet deep down this vantage point in time calls us to serious reflection—to review our lives and mission, to seek divine guidance, and to recommit our lives to our Lord as we enter the third Christian millennium.

One strain of thought that keeps ringing through my mind is that this should be made the occasion of great Christian celebrations all around the world.

There are several reasons for this. The first has to do with the spread of Christianity. More than at any time since Christ walked the shores of Galilee it can be seen that the gospel has appealed to peoples of almost every tribe and nation. And where it has entered, life has become fundamentally and proudly different.

The second is that this could now be made a wonderful occasion for Christians everywhere to praise God for the salvation made possible through Jesus Christ. Think how few could have worshiped God in celebration of the events of Calvary at the end of the first Christian millennium—how few knew about or used an anno Domini system of dating—and how wide was the world and isolated its peoples. Now, however, a worldwide concert of celebration of thanks to God is both a feasible possibility and could be a great missionary event.

On the other hand, all this makes us aware that the church

has not yet completed its mission on earth, and we are still here to fulfill God's purposes.

We come to this last chapter by turning our vision both backward and forward as we did at the outset. In the course of our studies we have given thought to various aspects of the church. Our investigations have ranged from theological thought about what the church is and what it has been called into being to do, to more sociological-like questions about relationships between members within the church and between the church and the world.

The church is the body of Christ. In some sense this remains a mystery that is inexplicable in the categories of ordinary human thought. Further, the church is the temple in which God is present in the Holy Spirit. Like our Master Himself during the Incarnation, there is that which is divine and that which is earthly about the church. It is composed of human beings, who are less than perfect, and as it makes its way in society its beauty is marred by human failings. And yet it is a sign, by the values it upholds and the relationships it sustains, of the kingdom of God. Frail and prone to human weakness, it shines with a light that illuminates it from above. Weak and feeble in an earthly sense, it holds within it the greatest power on earth. Small and beleaguered in many places, it is the greatest monument on earth.

We have thought of the nature and attributes of the church in these chapters; of its relationships, both internal and external; and of the tasks it has been called into being to perform—to nurture and challenge those within and to proclaim the message abroad. And we have been reminded all the while that the mysteries of God are beyond our comprehension. Now in this last chapter we turn our eyes forward to visions that are both turbulent and magnificent. We think of the glorious appearing of our Lord, of the time of trouble that precedes it, and of our heavenly home.

The Future—Four Vignettes

Scriptural passages portray four significant eschatological vignettes. God's Word reminds us of our present citizenship.

1. We walk the streets of this earth, yet we are citizens of heaven. 2. We must be vigilant, for the end is near. 3. There are troublous times ahead, but we are admonished not to cast away our confidence. 4. The kingdom to come will be exceedingly glorious.

We shall pay attention to each of these in four separate sections. The chapter will be brought to conclusion by turning the light back upon ourselves and our orientation to the tasks and glory that lie ahead.

Our Present Status—"Our citizenship is in heaven" (Phil. 3:20). There is a dual grounding to this. In the first instance, we are children of the Creator, made in the image of God. It is true, of course, that our natures are marred by our fall into sin, but deep down there has remained an inkling of who we are—an intimation, as it were, of the realm to which we truly belong. As Augustine was fond of saying: "Thou hast formed us for Thyself, and our hearts are restless till they find their rest in Thee."[1] In addition to this deep inclination toward higher things, we are citizens of heaven because of the atonement and our adoption in Jesus Christ. We are thus doubly citizens of the kingdom, and the human soul has a void that is not satisfied by things below.

The concept of the seeking soul is not merely a theoretical construct. One keeps running into reports of those who find life meaningless without a relationship with God. For instance, an article in the *Wall Street Journal* of April 10, 1998, with the title "More Professionals Return to Church or Synagogue; Having It All Isn't Enough" is not unusual. The article goes on to ask, "Can you go back?" On the one hand, this deep longing of the soul for something more is the secret ally of the evangelist. On the other hand, the great challenge to us at this time in history as citizens of both worlds, as this article points out, is to find a way of speaking to this need and promoting a climate within the church so that they can come back.

The End Is Near—Passages such as Luke 21:28-36, Matthew 24:32-44, and Matthew 25:1-13 relate many of the parables and admonitions of Jesus regarding the nearness of the end—parables of the fig tree, a thief in the night, two women at the mill, parallels with the days of Noah, and the wise and foolish bridesmaids. Each of these parables is etched in the Adventist experience, and belief in the nearness of His coming has been one of the defining principles of the movement. It has also been a driving force in the remarkable worldwide missionary expansion of the church. And concern for efficiency in the fulfillment of the eschatological mandate to mission has been a determining factor in the formation of church administrative and financial systems.

One has only to turn the pages of the *Review and Herald* of Battle Creek days, taking note of the articles written by the founders of the church, to get a feeling of the sense of urgency that inspired them. What moves me even more is the loving expectancy with which they looked forward to being with the Saviour.

Many early Advent hymns reflect the same concerns and hopes. Among these are several of the F. E. Belden gospel songs: "At the Door," "We Know Not the Hour," and "Let Every Lamp Be Burning," and Uriah Smith's "O Brother, Be Faithful." There is a haunting beauty to his sister Annie Smith's "How Far From Home?" and "Long Upon the Mountains." Their hopes and longings for a soon-coming Saviour have been at the very heart of Adventism since its inception.

Jesus concluded His telling of the parables of the kingdom, according to the Lukan narrative, with a warning that rings through the centuries with a relevant freshness. "Be on guard so that your hearts are not weighed down with dissipation . . . and the worries of this life. . . . Be alert at all times, praying that you may have the strength to escape all these things that will take place, and to stand before the Son of Man" (Luke 21:34-36).

Jesus' warning to His followers that they should take care that their hearts are not weighed down with the concerns of this life and that they should be alert at all times would seem to be even more relevant in the contemporary setting of our lives than it was when Jesus spoke originally. Faith was easier in those days, and life was simpler. Ours is a secular disbelieving age, and we are bombarded with distractions and beguiling information from every direction. When I read the words "be alert," they speak to me more about the state of my own mind and consciousness than about the external signs of the coming kingdom. One of the great challenges facing us today is that of keeping the blessed hope burning brightly before us as the goal to which all of life is geared.

Finally, we are reminded again that no one knows the hour of His coming. Signs there will be, but the days of time-setting are past. We should not attempt to predict when our Lord will come. He is the sovereign Lord of history and will come when His purposes on earth have been fulfilled. It is for us to live in the blessed hope and move among the human race with the radiance of that kingdom illuminating our lives and work to proclaim the gospel to all who have not heard.

In South Africa I was saddened about 30 years ago when visiting an old minister whom I had much admired. He had given his life and everything he had in single-minded devotion to the proclamation of the message and had fully hoped to be translated and caught up in the body to be with his Lord. It was the vision of his life. And there he was, a bitterly disappointed old man upon the brink of the grave, feeling that his Lord had let him down.

It is not for us to dictate to the Lord or to place our personal wishes for salvation and translation to a better world above God's purposes for the peoples and nations of the world. At times I detect on the part of some a narrowness about our eschatological hope that is reflected in a tendency to reduce the blessed hope to a matter of personal rewards rather than to see it as the culminating fulfillment of God's cosmic purposes.

Endure; Cast Not Away Your Confidence—Romans 8:18-23, 9:28, and Hebrews 10:35-37 remind us that there will be a time of great trouble in the days preceding the Second Advent. The time of trouble will be a major chapter in the conflict between the forces of good and evil. The prince of darkness in his anger will marshal forces against the saints of the Most High. Ellen White enlarges on this and gives us many solemn warnings, but she also gives repeated assurance that those whose hearts are fully consecrated to the Lord can rest assured in Him.[2]

There is a double basis for our assurance. In the first instance, our confidence is based upon Christ's work. The battle has already been won. Christ emerged from the grave the victor over the prince of darkness and death. In the second instance, we have confidence because of the Incarnation.

This takes us back to a consideration of the person of Christ. In some sense, Christ took our human nature upon Himself permanently. "Christ Jesus, himself human" is the one mediator between God and humankind (1 Tim. 2:5). Ellen White writes: "God gave his only begotten Son to become one of the human family, forever to retain His human nature."[3] This fact is a spectacular demonstration that the human race was not irrevocably doomed at the Fall. If there had been no possibility of restoration, Christ would not have taken our nature upon Himself. That He permanently took our nature is assurance that we will be with Him, "our elder brother" (see Heb. 2:11, 12, 17), in His kingdom. He identified Himself with us in the Incarnation in order that we might be identified with Him in His kingdom.

Our assurance is thus grounded in the person of Christ as well as in His work of atonement on the cross. A time of trouble there will be—but our hope is certain. Our reward is secure. There is no reason for lack of assurance or to cast away our confidence.

The Glories of the Kingdom of God—Isaiah 35:1-10, Isaiah 65:17-25, 1 Corinthians 2:9, Revelation 21:1-5, and Revelation 22:1-5 assure us of a glorious future. Isaiah presents us with portrayals of the descriptions of Zion as the culminating climax of the great Messianic march of the nations to the City of God. These are portrayals of what should have taken place had Israel been fully faithful in the fulfillment of God's purposes. As such, although these are but shadows of the eternal city, they give us glimpses of the wonders of the kingdom of heaven.

John the revelator presents us with the two most graphic and glorious presentations of the New Jerusalem in the Scriptures. But as Paul reminds us by quoting Isaiah 64:4, despite the detail and magnificence of these portrayals, the human heart cannot really conceive what God has prepared for those who love Him (1 Cor. 2:9).

Ellen White describes the personal richness of life in relationship to the heavenly community in an appeal to her readers. "The heart of God yearns over His earthly children with a love stronger than death. In giving up His Son, He has poured out to us all heaven in one gift. The Saviour's life and death and intercession, the ministry of angels, the pleading of the Spirit, the Father working above and through all, the unceasing interest of heavenly beings—all are enlisted in behalf of man's redemption.

"Oh, let us contemplate the amazing sacrifice that has been made for us! Let us try to appreciate the labor and energy that Heaven is expending to reclaim the lost, and bring them back to the Father's house. Motives stronger, and agencies more powerful, could never be brought into operation; the exceeding rewards for right-doing, the enjoyment of heaven, the society of the angels, the communion and love of God and His Son, the elevation and extension of all our powers throughout eternal ages—are these not mighty incentives and encouragements to urge us to give the heart's loving service to our Creator and Redeemer?

"And, on the other hand, the judgments of God pronounced against sin, the inevitable retribution, the degradation of our character, and the final destruction, are presented in God's Word to warn us again the service of Satan.

"Shall we not regard the mercy of God? What more could He do? Let us place ourselves in right relation to Him who has loved us with amazing love. Let us avail ourselves of the means provided for us that we may be transformed into His likeness, and be restored to fellowship with the ministering angels, to harmony and communion with the Father and the Son."[4]

I must confess that, as I read of the magnificence of that city and its beauty, it is not so much the physical attractions that move my heart as does contemplation of fellowship with the heavenly hosts and the redeemed.

In the same connection, the picture Ellen White portrays in *The Great Controversy* of the entry of the ransomed into the City of God, of the meeting of the two Adams, and of the great song of praise of the 144,000 is profoundly moving.[5]

An incident that is illustrative of the intimacy of the experience of salvation stands out in my memory. We celebrated the Lord's Supper at Solusi College in Zimbabwe one afternoon at the close of a series of meetings. It had been a long service. Nobody in that society comes lightly to partake of holy things. One's heart must be clean. If need be, confessions must be made and wrongs put right—sometimes publicly—before the meal. There had been some of this. And there were testimonies of joy and blessings. There was a radiance and happiness during the celebration at the Lord's table. It was now over. The closing song had been sung and the benediction pronounced. But the congregation lingered, reluctant to leave.

And then an old man stood up. There was to be another testimony. Everybody remained. What is time when sacred things are to be shared? With a quavering voice he told of earlier wanton ways, but now proclaimed that he was a follower of Christ. Then gloriously he spoke of the happiness of his heart. The Lord's Supper had been to him a foretaste of the feast we will celebrate with Christ in the city above.

Then he said, "You see these tears on my face? They are tears of happiness. When we enter that place, Jesus will welcome each one of us. We will come with tears of sadness and tears of joy, and Jesus Himself will wipe them away. He will not use a handkerchief or the sleeve of His robe. He will wipe the tears from our eyes with His own finger, as a mother does to a small baby, so that we can see. Then we will look into His eyes and see His love for us, and the beauty of His face."

His testimony inspired Ruth Gorle, a fellow member of the faculty, to write the following poem:

What tears?
    Not nature's kindly bath for eyes
Else blind with dust and strain;
    Not merry drops
From laughter's ripple;
    Not delight's quick gems.
The tears God wipes are sorrow's toll,
    Hard forced
By grip of grief, or pain, or fear, or dearth
Of hope; or agony of loss like His
That fell on Olivet.

How wiped away?
Shall God enfold our woe in His great arm
And with a kerchief finer than a cloud
Remove its burning sign?

Ah, no! No cloth,
Were it of heaven's weave,
    Shall wipe earth's tears.
Lit by God's smile, they shall become a mist,
A rainbow on the lash, the dew of dawn
Before the gold and sapphire blaze of day.[6]

A Covenant of Renewal

How can we best bring this book to a close? How can we best prepare ourselves and our church community for service in the new Christian millennium? Perhaps we should give consideration to a service of renewal.

This thought is inspired by the covenant renewal services John Wesley developed to strengthen and consolidate the people called Methodists. He drew on the personal covenant concept of the Puritans, in which persons bound themselves to certain duties, disciplines, and virtues, and he adapted it for corporate use. It was first celebrated in London in 1755 on a Sunday evening in August, but later it was regularly celebrated on the first Sunday of the new year.

At the first celebration Wesley recited the covenant featuring the words "I will be no longer mine own, but will give up myself to Thy will in all things." Eighteen hundred Methodists stood up in a "testimony of assent."

A later form of this covenant liturgy reads as follows:

The Covenant

"Then, the people standing, the minister shall say,

And now, beloved, let us bind ourselves with willing bonds to our covenant God, and take the yoke of Christ upon us.

"This taking of His yoke upon us means that we are heartily content that He appoint us our place and work, and that He alone be our reward.

"Christ has many services to be done; some are easy, others are difficult; some bring honor, others bring reproach; some are suitable to our natural inclinations and temporal interests, others are contrary to both. In some we may please Christ and please ourselves; in others we cannot please Christ except by denying ourselves. Yet the power to do all these things is assuredly given us in Christ, who strengthens us.

"Therefore let us make the covenant of God our own. Let us engage our heart to the Lord, and resolve in His strength never to go back.

"Being thus prepared, let us now, in sincere dependence on His grace and trusting in His promises, yield ourselves anew to Him.

"Here let the people kneel or bow, and the minister say in the name of all,

"O Lord God, holy Father, who hast called us through Christ to be partakers in this gracious covenant: We take upon ourselves with joy the yoke of obedience, and engage ourselves, for love of Thee, to seek and do Thy perfect will. We are no

156

longer our own, but Thine.

"Then all shall say,

"I am no longer my own, but Thine. Put me to what Thou wilt, rank me with whom Thou wilt; put me to doing, put me to suffering; let me be employed for Thee or laid aside for Thee, exalted for Thee or brought low for Thee; let me be full, let me be empty; let me have all things, let me have nothing; I freely and heartily yield all things to Thy pleasure and disposal.

"And now, O glorious and blessed God, Father, Son, and Holy Spirit, Thou art mine, and I am Thine. So be it. And the covenant which I have made on earth, let it be ratified in heaven. Amen."[7]

The Wesleyan covenant renewal service aggregates individual acts of covenant into a collective renewal of vows and dedication. It is typically Wesleyan in that personal decision-making is encouraged within the context of the spiritual pilgrimage of the community. Adventists are perhaps more inclined to emphasize personal spiritual pilgrimage within the context of corporate commitment to a world missionary task. The differences are at least partially a result of the Adventist eschatological focus that fosters zeal regarding the finishing of the work and personal incentive to be ready when He comes.

This covenant renewal service may not be entirely appropriate to an Adventist celebration marking the commencement of the third Christian millennium. We would want a more distinctly eschatological emphasis. And yet if we could build upon the concept, incorporating Adventist themes of mission and the nearness of the Second Coming, combining praise and rededication in a great celebration of renewal, it would be a wonderful way to enter the third millennium of our Lord.

---

[1] Augustine, *Confessions,* 1. 1. 1.
[2] See, for instance, "The Time of Trouble," *The Great Controversy* (Mountain View, Calif.: Pacific Press Pub. Assn., 1911), pp. 613-634.
[3] *The Desire of Ages,* p. 25.

[4] *Steps to Christ,* pp. 21, 22.

[5] *Ibid.,* pp. 646-648.

[6] Drusilla Hertogs, *Ruth Gorle: Makhumalo, Mother of Leaders* [self-published, 1996], p. 229.

[7] *The Book of Worship for Church and Home* (Nashville: The Methodist Publishing House, 1965), p. 387.